Michael Jackson
THE BOOK THE MEDIA DOESN'T WANT YOU TO READ

SHAWN HENNING

authorHOUSE®

AuthorHouse™
1663 Liberty Drive
Bloomington, IN 47403
www.authorhouse.com
Phone: 1-800-839-8640

© 2009 Shawn Henning. All rights reserved.

No part of this book may be reproduced, stored in a retrieval system, or transmitted by any means without the written permission of the author.

First published by AuthorHouse 9/25/2009

ISBN: 978-1-4490-3015-5 (e)
ISBN: 978-1-4490-3014-8 (sc)

Library of Congress Control Number: 2009909803

Printed in the United States of America
Bloomington, Indiana

This book is printed on acid-free paper.

CONTENTS

Introduction	3
Childhood	7
The Allegations	21
The Entertainer	37
The Humanitarian	49
Rebuilding Neverland	55
The Media	65
Statement	79
Personal Tribute	83
Illustrations and Tributes	85
Artists Sources	93
Other Sources	95

INTRODUCTION

I will begin by opening with two quotes from the father of science who in his time was accused of heresy, forced to recant, and spent the rest of his life under house arrest. Later, we learned he was right.

"In questions of science, the authority of a thousand is not worth the humble reasoning of a single individual." Galileo

"Where the senses fail us, reason must step in." Galileo

This is my humble reasoning and tribute to the King of Pop. This book will not contain interviews of highly prestigious actors, stars; make up artists, or even family members. It will not contain the opinions of highly paid doctors, attorneys, or even top forensic experts. Everything that can be written about Michael Jackson with those experts, has already been done, so much so that the truth about him has been lost in tainted journalism and, the truth is so far gone now that it might not ever be able to be recovered. I do not pretend to have some keen insight into the King of Pops controversial life, nor do I claim to have even been close to him or anyone that he knew. What I do offer is one fans point of view.

I have also been in touch with one defense witness for Michael Jackson this book will include some comments that he shared with me. It is worth, mentioning that he is a filmmaker, and has a completed documentary now available, entitled "The Untold Story of Neverland."

The media has done such a good job in opening the doors of Michaels life (be it the truth or misrepresentation of it) and exposing him that I feel almost as if Michael lived in the same house as me. This book intends to show Michael Jackson as the human being that he was and not the monster that the media created. I do hope that the message in these pages will provide enlightenment to those who seek the truth about the King of Pop.

I have complete respect for this Icon of music and with all the media stories and rumors about this legend, I felt as if the world should hear from a fan, an unbiased fan. I think Michael Jackson loved his fans and even turned to us to find some joy and protection from the media who had a field day with his name and life. I hope that this book will help the world see Michael from the viewpoint of his true fans, and just maybe between the media's coverage, interviews, and books written about him we can uncover what is true and what was biased opinion from media powerhouses.

Who is Michael Jackson? I have come across this question several times in my search for truth. His death, for some reason, has awoken in me a need to find out as much as I possibly could, about the man whose music I grew up listening too. I really can't explain why I felt a need to do this, but I think it's partly because the more I read the more stories and videos, the interviews and case facts, that I read the more it becomes, apparent that Michael Jackson's story has not been told in a way that had made any sense. Most of what I found was a biased view by people who stood to gain, something by tearing this man down. I read so much about Michael Jackson, and the positive things, were hidden and not easily accessible.

So many facts about the allegations that were never discussed among the major media players. So much of Michael Jackson never made open to the public in the same way they used to put in our heads this "monster," and a "freak." To the depth of my soul, it hurt to uncover some of the things that I did. If what I read is true, then we are in a world of trouble and we have to raise the question, whether or not our media is to be trusted. How many lies have been, told to us and, like sheep, how much of it have we believed? When do we say, enough is enough and when do we hold our media responsible for what is being shown? Finally, how many lives have already been destroyed, due to the media and its falsehoods?

We have all witnessed, many people telling us to be careful about what we watch and what we believe. Many famous people have proclaimed to the world that the media does not always paint a picture of truth. These pages are an attempt to bring some light to facts that were not included in the media's portrayal of Michael Jackson, the way they should have been. Instead, we now see a burning Michael Jackson on TV and reports that this led to his addiction to drugs. Even in death, the media has not finished burning Michael Jackson. Instead of detailing the doctors role in his PRESCRIPTION drug addiction they show a man burning and say this is the reason Michael was addicted to drugs.

As a fan I have a very different view, Instead of taking one tragic event lets look at several things that more likely helped in Michael's addiction. The media's coverage and refusal to tell the truth added to Michael Jackson addiction and "need to sleep." Just for a second lets talk about Martin Bashir's documentary a man who befriended and then betrayed Michael who later went on to admit that he never saw anything that was criminal. Could this have added to Michaels "drug addiction?" The kids that drug Michael to a court battle with some major life changing allegations.

Of course, most of what I have said up to this point is merely speculation save the part on Martin Bashir. However, most of the things told about Michael Jackson seem based on speculation and very little fact. In this book, I will discuss many different aspects of Michael Jackson all of which from a fans point of view. I do hope you his fans will enjoy an unbiased view of the King of Pop.

It is my intention to show the Michael Jackson's legacy, as it should be. This book will dispel the media's rumors and twisting of facts. Michael Jackson was much more than an entertainer he was a true humanitarian and the media refuses to show that instead they make profit by these rumors and lies. Controversy sells and the media used that to destroy an innocent man, who believed in giving all that he could to bettering the world we live in.

To his family I say that many people mourn his loss around the world and so many of us truly believe in his innocence, and appreciate the endless music and entertainment he has left us with. I for one did not have the honor in knowing Michael Jackson the way that you did, but my heart is truly with you as are in my thoughts and prayers. The media did not paint for us a true picture of Michael Jackson and I wish the world could have known him the way you did. In Loving Memory of one of the worlds greatest, I dedicate this book to the Family and Fans of The King of Pop, Michael Jackson.

CHILDHOOD

Michael Jackson had a love for children that prevented him from ever hurting a child. The media made it into something other than what it was. Peter Pan, a boy that never grew up was Michael Jackson. He had a strict upbringing and career at an early age that caused him to miss a lot of things a normal childhood would have, but as a grown up he would make sure that he lived his lost childhood.

"Children show me in their playful smiles the divine in everyone. This simple goodness shines straight from their hearts and only asks to be lived." Michael Jackson

"I love my family very much. I wish I could see them a little more often than I do. But we understand because we're a show business family and we all work." Michael Jackson

One area of Michael Jackson's life that has been a highlight reel for the media to eat up and pick apart was Michael Jackson's childhood. In an interview conducted by Martin Bashir, Michael Jackson spoke of an unsettling childhood. One in which he and his brothers had been beaten by their father, one in which Michael did not have friends and was always working and did not get much time to play. Bashir painted a truly horrific picture of Michael's childhood. In the "Take two interview the Footage You Were Never Meant to See," put out by Michael Jackson, in response to Bashir's documentary, the picture was a little different. Michael refers to his father as a genius.

The media has made a definite point to establish Joseph Jackson as an abusive money hungry father. Was Joseph Jackson abusive? Again, this is speculation but let us look at the facts that I stumbled across.

An article came out the day after Martin Basher's documentary aired; written by *Fox News* entitled "Michael Jackson's Unacceptable Behavior Revealed," in this article they said Michael also hated his mother for allowing this "abuse" to happen. However, Michael Jackson's will, tells another story. He left 40% to her, he even gave custody of his children to her, and she is still married to the "abusive" Joseph Jackson. Jackson mother gave an interview where she said Joseph would whip the kids but he never beat them. If Michael had enough trust for his mom to leave her in charge of his children's welfare and assists then maybe we should trust her own words.

Truth is we may not ever know what it was really like for Michael Jackson growing up but as a fan if watching him perform as a child and listening to those who worked with him is any indication to how Michael felt about his childhood then the media once again has informed us wrong. Michael Jackson has some home videos that you can watch through youtube.com in which he talks about how much he enjoyed entertaining and singing.

Berry Gordy said that Michael was inquisitive of all facets of the music industry and would choose to come to the studio instead of play outside. He was always asking questions and really wanted to know the business. We also know that Michael was a great entertainer even as a child. Performing is what he did and he loved it. You do not get to where he was as an artist by not enjoying what you do.

Now a critic may contest my story by saying Michael Jackson admitted on camera that his father had abused him. I will say this and again I am not an expert by any means on child abuse or behavior patterns but I have a theory that could explain some of Michael Jackson's comments about his father.

Michael Jackson...

Image provided by Fahad AlZayed of Kuwait

The media overplayed the fact that Michael said he was afraid from his father even to the point where he would faint or throw up. Let us talk about that for a moment. Name me a child who grew up in that period who was not afraid of their father when it came to receiving disciplined. I can remember in my own case when my mother would put me in the room when I had done something wrong and said wait until your father gets home. I would feel like I was going to pass out and remember feeling nauseous in the pit of my stomach.

I was born years after Michael and in my time discipline consisted of whoopings and sometimes with something, we called a switch back then. I can remember my father telling me to pick a branch from a tree in the backyard so that I could receive my discipline.

Now in Michael Jackson's time discipline was even more so. In that time it was more accepted for a child to get disciplined examples; schools allowed a child to be disciplined in school in most cases the principle would discipline the child. In those times if your child acted up in public it was not necessarily the parent or a family member who disciplined that child. Parents were a little harder on their children back then because it was acceptable by society.

As Michael grew older, he began to wonder what a "normal" childhood would have been like. He let his longing to have known about a "normal" childhood show in the way he lived his life. He developed a plutonic relationship with children so that he could live that childhood through them. His love for children allowed him to live through them and spent the better part of his life doing as much as he could for them. The way he saw children expressed in this quote

"I see God in a child's face...," Michael Jackson.

Michael Jackson...

Now his love for children resulted in a belief of a different kind of discipline one without hitting, or tree branches, or belts, or spanking and he made his belief in discipline known when he said "I would slit my own wrists before I hurt a child," in the Take Two footage.

Now, his father has a different view of discipline after all, he was raised in a different time when spanking you child was acceptable and very common form of discipline. Michael did not see it that way and developed a natural resentment to that discipline when he grew up and lived his life through children and he spoke out about it in Bashir's documentary. Simple concept really In Michael's eyes to spank a child was abuse and even our society has come to that belief and has made spanking your child a crime.

Two keys that we are missing because the media never went in to detail about them, is the fact that Michael forgave his father, which he stated in the Take Two footage and considered him a genius. The other fact when Michael passed left custody of his own children to his mother who has stated that Joe Jackson was not abusive. Therefore, I do not think I buy the abused child scenario, at least, not the way the media portrayed it.

What did the media have to gain by making it seem worse than it was? Again, you can look to the same fox news article for that answer. I will quote it directly. "I thought Michael Jackson said something interesting toward the beginning of last night's interview. He said, voluntarily, Just because you've been abused it doesn't make you an abuser. It was an early justification, I thought."

By giving the image that Michael was an abused child, it would make the horse pill that the media was feeding us easier to swallow. It made it easier for us to accept, that if he were an abused child, then naturally, he would abuse children. In order to make this kind of story believable, the media had to give the demon an origin, something to say where this behavior came from. Forget the facts of Michaels own children, and were he wanted his children to be in the event of his passing, forget the fact that he labeled his father a genius. If the media can put an image in our heads, that Michael had suffered abuse then that makes their claim even more real.

Something the media has not shown is the great parents the Jackson's had to have been. Every one of their nine children is a success story, that is something to be very proud of, and something the media has a duty to report, instead reported controversy. As a fan I would like to take a minute to show the commitment to their children's success, and the drive they had to have to bring them out of very hard times. If not for their continued dedication and commitments, we may not have had the privilege to enjoy so much entertainment that we have thus far. Not just from Michael, but from the entire Jackson Family. Each one of them has tremendous talent, and brought enjoyment to our lives. This is a great accomplishment and Michael let the world know it when he called Joseph Jackson a genius.

Webster's dictionary defines genius as "extraordinary intellectual power especially as manifested in creative activity." I have heard no reporter discuss the reason why Michael would call his "abusive" father a genius and I think discussing that would provide a better understanding of their relationship and more insight into the man Joseph Jackson. Since the world is speculating on allegations of abuse in Michael's early beginnings, let me provide an alternative picture.

Joseph Jackson very possibly saw the best in his kids and very much wanted the best for them and pushed them to be the best. Look at the time when the kids were growing up understand how difficult it was for this family at this era in the United States. Was racism a major factor in our society? Was opportunity equal for everyone? Is it possible the Jackson Family had enough love for their children to push them to be great?

Michael Jackson broke boundaries with his music that had not been broke before. His video Billie Jean aired on a station that had not played black entertainers up to that point. Michael created songs that brought Artists from different types of music together to raise money for poverty-stricken Africa. The love of the Jackson family showed in Michaels love for the world. Later in this book I will take a look at the Entertainer but it is crucial to mention some of this now so that we can see Joseph Jackson's work as a "genius," begin to unfold.

Michael Jackson...

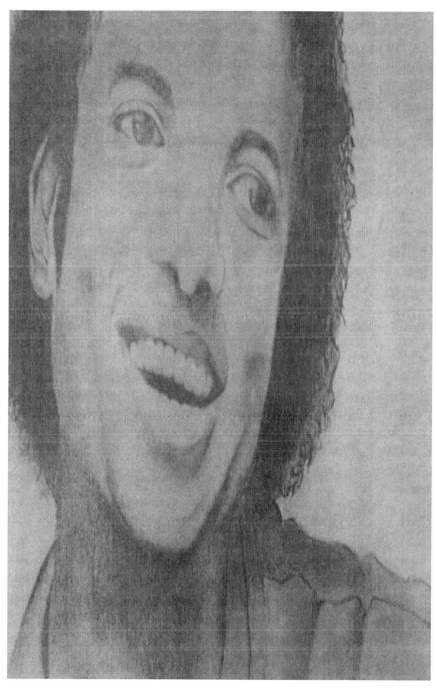

Drawing Provided by Kristina Farkas of Croatia

Michael grew up in a time when African Americans did not have as much as an opportunity as Caucasians I could only imagine what obstacles this family had to overcome in order to be where they are. Again as a fan, I thank the Jackson family for having the ability to overcome, to break barriers, and to help us as a society get to where we can accept one another as equals. Allegations of abuse have been a direct result of yellow journalism and in a time when we are suffering as a country, it takes that kind of commitment to our families to overcome and the Jackson Family should act as a beacon for all of us to follow.

Michael Jackson grew up in a large loving family, evidence of this very apparent in his home videos. A family that in his death stood and hugged every person that spoke at Michaels Memorial. We see a family that stood together and was not shy to express their love openly to each other, to the people who came and to the fans. This is not the making of an abusive family. Take the smallest thing as them standing together in a painstaking time and watch the love they expressed. This kind of Love is a moral instilled in children by their parents.

Love, that, they shared with the entire world, in a sad and grievous time. Why would the Jackson's allow us to share this time with them? Has no one asked that question? Could it be a dark conspiracy that the media would have us believe? Just maybe it was something less complicated something that we can sum up in one word, love. Love that they had for Michael, love and understanding that Michael loved his fans and we loved him.

Michael's childhood was that of a dream for all children. I cannot think of a child who would not have wanted to be Michael in that time. The Jackson 5 are a testament to a family's ability to see the best in themselves and to use that beautiful talent to overcome so much, not only their lives but even to pass that ability to overcome onto future generations, they made us believe anything was possible. The Jackson Five were not just some phase that swept the nation but they indeed crossed borders and oceans and the world over was blessed to have heard and watch this very talented family.

Michael went on to do so much for music, which inspired many stars in their careers, Justin Timberlake, Usher, Chris Tucker and many others. The mark he left for the music world is clear and without question. Through this reasoning, we can understand why Michael Jackson would call his father a genius because he was.

By calling him a genius, we can clearly see that Michael had a deeper respect and love for the man who made all this possible, deeper than any accusation of abuse. For the media to not paint this picture clearly shows they did not do their job and saw and printed only what they wanted to. Controversy sells and the media used that every chance they had. From Childhood to death, the media has surrounded this man and his family into controversy, and the message of pure love, dedication and commitment has been lost.

In Martin Bashir's "Living with Michael Jackson" so much of that interview was cut and edited and gave the world a view of Michael that was not accurate. Michael came back with the entire uncut interview in his "Take Two the Footage You Were Never Meant To See," and dispelled a lot of the views that were expressed by Bashir but unfortunately the Take two version did not get as much air time or discussion as Bashir's, the media did not scrutinize Bashir as they should have. If the image Bashir gave us is wrong then it is up to us to search what is truth. I believe Michael Jackson's life was very different from the biased views we have seen.

If the media can take Michael Jackson words about his father's alleged abuse and make the case that it happened and that Michael was beat as a child then why did they not give so much attention to what the other kids had to say.

"Yes our parents were strict, they did whip us, but my parents never mentally or sexually abused us." Janet Jackson

"I've come to realize that as we get older, we grow and learn a lot more. And I think that my father and my mother, they raised children the best way they know how," La Toya Jackson.

In addition, I should mention she said this after having gone through a very abusive relationship that the mainstream media did not choose to cover. The media not only attacked Michael, but they attacked his family and La Toya suffered a very traumatic experience but instead of revealing this to the public, the media added more controversy to this family at La Toya's expense.

It is worthy of noting, that out of nine children only two claimed that abuse occurred by father Joseph Jackson. Those two were Michael Jackson and La Toya Jackson and La Toya later made the comment that I previously quoted.

I think that we should mention a little more about La Toya Jackson as she is the only other child who claimed to have been abused and what she says could sway the public on this belief that there was or wasn't abuse in the Jackson family.

In 1994, La Toya gave *Eyewitness News* an interview claiming that Michael's ever-changing face was because he did not want to look like his father; she also said that their family was dysfunctional and that Michael and her, used to play a game where they would ask each other if something happened to Joe Jackson would they cry.

This was the Medias story and at the end of the broadcast, the reporting journalist says, "No doubt the Jackson family saga will continue." I mention this because a few disturbing facts about La Toya's marriage at this time would reveal that she was made to say these things against her will by her husband Jack Gordon, whom she later divorced and sued for years of abuse.

A lot has been said about La Toya save the fact that previously being married to Jack Gordon, La Toya was a girl with strong morals so strong infact she reportedly once dropped a friend who had begun wearing low-cut tops and skirts with slits in them. After her marriage with Gordon, we saw a very different La Toya.

The Jackson kids contrary to media opinion were raised with high morals and commitment to the future. It takes a lot of commitment and love for parents to keep their children on the right track, and instead of praising a family who did exactly that, we instead, tear them down with baseless allegations and rumors. Journalism designed to keep the "Jackson family saga" an ongoing event.

Michael Jackson...

As a fan of the Jackson's I do not see it as a saga but more as a families struggle and commitment to being the best. I would venture to say that the Jackson's upbringing is far from abusive and tell their story with that kind of journalism is outrageous and immoral. This family is a success story and the only controversy I have found is that of the medias' blatant attacks and portrait of the Jackson Family. I found an interesting article that shows the Jackson's at a young age. I will take it systematically as it a very informative about the Jackson family, written in 1972, a little different from what we heard in Bashir's documentary/interview and the media reports.

I found a newspaper clipping dated July 22 1972; in my search for truth, this article would provide me an interesting insight into Michael Jackson at the age of twelve. The article from the *Free-Lance Star* shows us a view far different from what the current media would like us to believe. I will to take some time to show some things from this article because in my opinion has useful insights to the child Michael Jackson, his childhood, the entertainer and the way that Michael felt about love even back then.

The article written by Mary Campbell started by saying "We went to interview the Jackson five one morning and found six." Then would go on to name the Jackson's, Jackie, Tito, Jermaine, Marlon, Michael, and Randy. They would then note what Michael was wearing "Michael was wearing a T-Shirt with the word Love written on it." Jermaine Jackson would report, "He wears them on every tour, it's his traveling T-shirt."

The article would then talk about Michael's solo album coming out on *Motown* "Got to be there," they mentioned a single from it "Got to be where you are." The next part of the article I found very interesting, they asked Michael about singing love songs at a young age, his reply was "its not odd for me to sing about love songs because I know what I am singing about," His brothers laughed at Michaels comment with brother Jackie saying "He gets really deeply involved."

The article would go on to discuss the Jackson 5 success and albums and how they got started. The article would talk about their shows, and how they spent one Christmas performing at the Apollo Jackie said,

"That's what we wanted to do. We were just getting started so we were a little anxious."

"Then the article discusses Michael, being the first to have a solo album, and how all the brothers planned to do the same; brother Marlon playfully added, "Mine will be like Michaels." The article moved on to talk about how they enjoyed motorcycles, "except for Jackie who had a Camero." Jermaine chimed in saying he "would be getting his car soon."

Then the reporters asked the boys if their father was strict? The article reported, "We hear both yes and no. I found Michaels comment to be extremely important given the alleged abuse. "We have a tutor that travels with us, when were at home we go to a regular school, private school. Our father travels with us to see that everything goes right."

Jackie then says "we all have to do our chores around the house like every other kid would do and we get out once in a while but basically everything is like everyone else."

Then the kids sang the theme song for the movie "Ben" for the reporters. They go on to joke with each other more as they tell the reporters about Michaels rubber rat that he brings on tour. The article concludes as they ask about fighting between the brothers "we just like to play, they're brotherly love fights."

The article is very different from how the media has portrayed Michael and the Jackson Family. Here it shows that Michael had a deep belief in love so much so he carried it with him on every tour. It shows a very playful Jackson family and not the rumored jealousy of each other, it also shows that they believed there life was almost normal and they were happy to be where they were. It showed the Jackson kids making plans for cars with one already having a vehicle sounds to me like Father, Joseph Jackson, was not so abusive that he kept his children without some of the finer things.

Another interesting fact is that Michael Jackson had father Joe Jackson as his Manager until around 1980. In 1980, Joe Jackson would show us his human side and admit he had been having an affair, an affair that would produce a child. It was then, that Michael would become distant from his father and the family. This is in my opinion the main reason why Michael would say harsh things about his father.

Michael would feel hurt and betrayed by his father's admissions and he would never fully recover from it. Michaels own words as a child was that his father was always there to make sure things had gone right but with Joe's admission, it was clear that things were not all right and this would scar Michael. It is not incomprehensible for a child to develop resentment for his father with this kind of confession. It happens all the time in average families.

Not all was lost however in years to come we would see signs of a bond that was still there, signs that make me dispute the allegations of Joe Jackson being a money hungry father who beat his children. Michael would go through some of the most difficult times in his life in 1993 and then again in 2003. Father Joseph Jackson would be there in Michael's darkest hours, supporting him. Not quite the abusive father the media has led us to believe.

In reasoning, we can see Michael at a young age loved entertaining also, we can see that he felt strongly about the word love. We can also see that as a star, his life was a little different from average kids but it was not as isolated as the media would have us believe. Michael may have had a stricter upbringing than most because it is clear that father Joseph Jackson wanted the best for his kids and he kept them focused. However, strict as he was, he still kept his kids with some of life's pleasantries cars and toys. Is this the "abusive father," the media is refers to?

In Bashir's Interview Michael Jackson said, "There was no Christmas as a child." Is that because, the father was so abusive, that he did not allow his kids celebrate Christmas, or is it simply because the families' religion did not believe in celebrating Christmas? Here we see the medias' twisting of the truth to paint an image of abuse. If the media can bend the truth and show it, as they want us to see it. Then what else, have they twisted to fit their stories?

Michael Jackson did endure a difficult childhood but not in the way, the media claims. Reasoning will tell us that Michael grew up in a time that consisted of racism and prejudice. It was difficult for minorities to achieve their dreams back then. Michael's family would accept nothing less than the best for their nine children. The Jackson family pushed their children to be the best they could be, not in the way the media shows, but in the way that showed commitment to providing their children with the best opportunities.

Simple logic tells us that the media's stories are false. They never produced one photograph that showed any sign of abuse. What we see is a smiling, playful Michael Jackson who enjoyed entertaining. Logic also tells us that Michael grew up in hard times and his parents wanted more for their children. They pushed their children to succeed and this is why Michael labeled his father as a genius.

If we use our common sense, we can see that Michael had his father as his manager until 1980, when Joseph admitted to an affair that also bared a child. It was then that Michael released Joseph as his manager and not before. It was then that he began to distance himself from his father. Although, the admission hurt the bond they shared, we also saw that bond strong enough to bring them together, when Michael would face outlandish allegations in 1993 then again in 2003.

THE ALLEGATIONS

What does the word love mean? There are several definitions of love, I found one that I felt best described Michael Jackson use of the word when he referred to children. *Webster's Dictionary* gives us this definition of the word love: "unselfish loyal and benevolent concern for the good of another."

> *"Everyone who knows me will know the truth, which is that my children come first in my life and that I would never harm any child...." Michael Jackson*

> *"Let us dream of tomorrow where we can truly love from the soul, and know love as the ultimate truth at the heart of all creation..." Michael Jackson*

In the first chapter, I tried to give an image of Michaels Jackson's belief in the word love, and how that belief, turned feelings of a strict upbringing into an alleged abuse allegation against Michael's father. I tried to show that any physical disciplinary act on a child Michael would have referred to it as abuse. I also tried to paint a picture of the Michael Jackson family in a way that mainstream failed to do, as a loving but strict family who cared enough for their children to push them to succeed.

The first chapter is crucial in understanding this chapter, intended to show Michaels belief in love simply would not allow him to commit an act as horrifying as molestation. In addition, it was to dispel the medias rumors, that Michael suffered abuse and therefore abused children. This chapter is the horse pill I referred to in the first chapter. I pray that this puts out the information his fans across the world have been saying for years.

The mainstream media ignored so many facts about the cases, and the facts they reported were twisted for personal gain. . Michael, your fans know the truth, and whatever mainstream media tries to say, we believe in you, and we will continue to push to make people see the truth. In your life, they did not make the truth known and now even in your passing they still refuse to state the facts and leave you with a title that you should never have had.

Let us explore each case individually and discover what the media did not report. These allegations broke Michael's heart and forever labeled him in the minds of sheep as a pedophile, his fans across the world have a very different view.

1993, Jackson is accused by Evan Chandler father of then 13yr Jordon Chandler. The media ran ramped with stories and rumors, as if Michael was already convicted. Images of Neverland show the home no longer a place of innocence, where children could play, but a much darker image of Neverland is casted by media stories. The place were children from all walks of life came, laughed, and played for free, now tainted by police raids and ghastly stories of innocence lost forever.

A year prior to this accusation, Evan Chandler reportedly invited Michael to build an extended wing to their home so that the singer could move in with them. A drastic difference in the allegations he would make a year later, why the change of heart? Evan Chandler by his own admission according to Wikipedia was jealous of the relationship that Michael had with his son. This jealousy in my opinion would set a plan in motion to extort Michael for money.

This allegation was not about Jordon Chandler who if was molested, that is all this case should have been about, but seeing as how Jordon Chandler refused to testify against Michael. Evan Chandler, his father takes center stage in this allegation. Let us take a closer look at Mr. Chandler.

Is Evan Chandler the caring father who sought justice for his abused son? Do many caring fathers owe $68,000 worth of back child support? Evan Chandler was a respected dentist so money could not be the reason for his not paying child support. So why would this caring father not pay for his own children? Interesting question and I wish I had the answer but the media never discussed it.

The media instead, would have us believe that Evan was a caring and loving father who was concerned about the welfare of his child. However in a taped conversation he was asked about the affects all of this was having on his poor son Jordon Chandler, I will quote his very loving response, "That's irrelevant to me...It will be a massacre if I don't get what I want." The love for his children made clear in this recorded interview.

There is of course the medical attention he provided for his son to help him remove a tooth. This is a caring act or at least it would be had he not given his son a sedative called sodium Amytal whose effects are known to make patients open for suggestion. Under the influence of this drug, Jordon Chandler makes his accusations against Michael.

Jordon Chandler claimed that he could describe Jackson's genitals. However, after 25-minute examination, photographs proved there were inconsistencies in Jordon's description including a claim of circumcision, a vital piece in identifying a mans genitals, I would think.

Jordon Chandler's story of the abuse was co-oberated by witnesses, employed by Michael Jackson at the time of the alleged incident. Most of which sold their stories to the tabloids, instead of going to police. I have heard from unnamed sources that the Chandlers supposedly paid money to the witnesses that did go to the police. Although I could not substantiate the report, Michael Jackson did successfully sue many of those witnesses, later in separate courts.

Therefore, we have the very loving father Evan Chandler who clearly sought justice for his victimized son and we have the reliable witnesses who sold there stories to tabloids and media powerhouses like *Hard Copy* for handsome sums of money. We also have the fact that Neverland, played hosts to thousands of children a year, and out of thousands, Michael Jackson came under investigation twice.

Surely, with a case of this magnitude other children would have stepped forward to address the allegations. In fact, the prosecution claimed many children had been molested; here is what happened with those claims.

Jason Francia was the son of a house cleaner who worked at Neverland. Jason claimed that Michael Jackson had touched his penus twice. His mother Blanca Francia also made claims that she had seen Michael Jackson with a boy in the shower. She would later admit in court that she did not see anything. As for Jason's claims they were discredited when it was proven that the mother had been fired two years before in 1991 and was not even working at the ranch when these claims were supposed to have had happened.

Macaulay Culkin, the child superstar, whom the prosecution also claimed was molested. Strongly denied these allegations and actually testified in court on behalf of Michael Jackson.

Wade Robson and Brett Barnes also children the prosecution claimed were molested, also testified in court on behalf of Michael Jackson, both denying that Michael had ever touched them.

With all these, "reliable" witness's only one child ever testified against Michael and he was discredited in court. The main accuser, Jordon Chandler, refused to testify not once but twice once in 1993 and then again years later in 2003. After Michaels death false internet reports claimed that Jordon Chandler had finally come forward to admit that Michael Jackson was innocent. The reports were a fabrication but it was Michael Jackson's fans plea to Jason, to honor Michael Jackson's death and finally admit the truth.

To me this case seems more like a media vulture circus than a search for truth. A 13yr old boy had allegedly been molested, but instead of searching for the truth, the media and alleged witnesses saw a chance to get paid and took advantage of an innocent man guilty of one thing, kindness.

With all this "reliable," information, it was a shock when the state closed its case against Michael saying there was a lack of evidence. Let's think about that for a moment, the state closed its case against Michael Jackson, saying there was a lack of evidence that supported these allegations. The way the media had portrayed Michael was as if he was already guilty, and Michael was a sick perverted freak, what was the name they gave him oh yes Wacko Jacko.

Sounds to me like an open and shut case, but instead of the media focusing on the state closing the case and proclaiming the man innocent, the frustrated media found salvation in a civil suit. Michael Jackson had elected to pay the sum of 22 million out of court. The news shocked the world and even me. With everything going, his way why would he settle out of court?

One source I found gave a good reason for this payoff, "Eventually Presley, Taylor, and Jackson's team all agreed that the singer should settle out of court; it was their opinion that the entertainer's health had deteriorated to such a degree that he could not endure a lengthy trial."

Michael Jackson health was a large concern for the people who took control of Michael's legal defenses and finances. Michael Jackson was seeking medical help at this time because he was not in good shape. Michael had become addicted to prescription drugs; he was suffering weight loss, was not eating properly, and was not sleeping at all. Reports that he could not remember details about his music and albums and slurred speech was cited in a separate court.

After this trial the secretary for the prosecution would write and publish a book, it was her account of what happened in that trial and in the prosecutors' office. She claimed the allegations were a set up to extort an innocent man for money.

Millions of fans around the world proclaim his innocence and believe that the media did not report the truth. One investigative reporter wrote a book as well claiming she had been caught up in the medias' portrayal of Michael Jackson and was guilty of it to, but her book was a dedication to Michael to try to set the record straight.

This case hurt Michael to his very core. The media coverage and the allegations were more than Michael could bear. While the media and the Chandler family took pride in what they were doing, Michael Jackson was dying from the inside. The allegation had taken its toll on Michael and his music. Many songs that came out after this case seemed to have been directed at the media and the prosecuting attorney. Michael Jackson lost endorsements and songs recorded for a specific movie were dropped. His albums sales were there but it was clear, a piece of Michael Jackson's innocence had been lost.

Even with all this, the media to this day has forever labeled Michael a freak, a sideshow, Wacko Jacko and his payout to the Chandler family was quickly made public and Michael Jackson was guilty to the world. Despite the fact, the case was shut down due to lack of evidence. Despite all the unreliable witnesses, the prosecution had provided.

In this section, my intention is to show that settlements in Hollywood are common and most entertainers choose to do this just to make the problem go away and avoid scandal.

Entertainers are very busy and even if they are innocent, they elect to pay because they do not have the time for a drawn out trial that the media might make into a circus. We all know that the life of an entertainer is not a normal life. With the Paparazzi and other media influences detailing every second of your life and everything an entertainer might do. Entertainers know that the media will more than likely report rumors instead of what is true. Often times an entertainer may have to deal with whatever scandal for the rest of their life.

Things that seem common to regular people are a scandal in the entertainer world. We have to be reasonable; the media cover even the most natural of things like pregnancy very close. Even though we as average people know this we still listen to the media when they accuse Michael of strange acts by covering his kids faces and find ourselves agreeing with them that wow that is strange, forget the fact that we do not have to deal with the same things entertainers do.

I wanted to bring to light some other entertainers that allegedly made payouts. I do not intend to go into details of their cases because this book is not about them. I will say this though, entertainers will always be subject to lawsuits, and scandals because frankly people become jealous of these entertainers and when given the opportunity will try to take something from these entertainers. Whether we believe in these entertainers' innocence or not reality is these people, have money and there are some people who would love a free ride and would do or say, just about anything, to get apiece of what is not rightfully theirs.

- Bill Cosby (allegedly)
- Kobe Bryant (who was proven innocent still allegedly paid a settlement)
- Ashanti (allegedly)
- OJ Simpson (who even though was proven innocent had to pay in civil judgment)
- Robert Blake (who was also acquitted of charges but had to pay in a civil judgment

There are many others some we know about and some we do not. Some of these entertainers will forever be marked as criminals and in two cases a murderer. Settlements are common practice in Hollywood be it a small case or a scandal that shocks the world. The point here is just because a star pays a settlement does not make him/her guilty. We can not judge on something we don't have a clue about, living that life is far different from our own it is a world built on drama and scandals, it is a world that whatever an entertainer does affects everything about them including children that they may have.

With the case closed and Michaels settling, the circus was finally over. Although for Michael and the media, it never really was over. The people had been given an image of Michael that would never go away. However, Michael did try to move on with his life and his music. He would get married to Lisa Marie Presley and go on to make many albums. In 2003, Michael would again come under microscope as new allegations emerged.

More than ten years had passed since Jordon Chandler and his father Evan Chandler had made the allegations of molestation. Michael Jackson would never forget the year 1993 but he did try to move on a put this behind him. Unfortunately that would not happen and Michael was about to be put into the fire again.

Prior to the allegations, in 2003, a documentary/interview by a Martin Bashir aired on television, "Living with Michael Jackson." The interview was made under the pretenses to show the truth about Michael Jackson. Instead, it created a very disturbing image of Michael and only confirmed what the mainstream media had being saying all along. The media pet name Wacko Jacko was front and center in this video. The video made it seem as if all the rumors about Michael were true and it would have been that way had Michael not released the unedited version of the interview, "Take Two the Footage You Were Never Meant to See".

Bashir's version created a vision of the abused, plastic surgery addicted, crazed father Michael Jackson. It created a terrifying image of Neverland one that would rival the scariest of haunted houses. Michael's version taped during Bashir's interview, with Bashir's knowledge, showed a very different view, and showed the two different opinions of Bashir himself. Bashir would publicly criticize Michael and Neverland but to Michaels face and Michael's cameras, Bashir would praise Michael and Neverland.

The biggest part of the Bashir documentary, were images of a boy by the name of Gavin Arvizo. A boy that had been diagnosed with cancer and whom Michael befriended, a boy that Michael not only helped to get through his traumatic ordeal but also gave money to help in is medical treatments. Gavin in Bashir's interview was shown holding hands with Michael, he placed his head on Michaels shoulder and told the world how they slept in the same bedroom together.

The images were disturbing and caused concern especially since Michael was an alleged pedophile. Bashir would say in the video that this concerned him deeply but Michael's version Bashir would praise Michael again for having that kind of love for a child. Bashir's video caused uproar and media powerhouses began to take center stage again feeding the masses the usual Wacko Jacko Image.

Is he wacko? Yeah, he's strange....*Fox News*

"Insight into 'disturbing' Michael Jackson" was the title for an article by *CNN*

The Guardian would say a better title for this documentary would be "living with schizophrenia."

"Michael Jackson is a disturbing individual..." *TVNZ*

WorldNet Daily published this complete lie "According to Jackson, not only do children like to be touched, but the superstar told Bashir he would kill himself if he could not be close to young boys."

"This is a 44-year-old man who yearns to be Peter Pan and who apparently has no one in his life who can tell him that's both impossible and unhealthy." *USA Today*

I found dozens of articles published by known media powerhouses and some smaller less known media sources. The media was at it again, beginning the conviction of Michael Jackson before he was charged with a crime.

Just to show you how biased the media was on Michael Jackson the Bashir Interview was aired over a dozen times on *ABC* alone, its ratings were; in the UK airing had 15 million viewers, while 38 million watched the two hour special on ABC. While the unedited version, was seen by only 2 million people, and aired once by a notable talk show host Maury.

I mention Bashir's documentary because it is vital to this case, many people believe it is the reason there was even a case, without it no allegations would ever had been made and I am one of those believers. Proof of this is found in Michael's unedited version with the entire Arvizo family praising Michael claiming no molestation ever occurred and evening threatening to sue Bashir.

Another thing I should mention before we get into the details of this case. Gavin and Michael had been friends for years prior to Bashir's footage aired in 2003; no claim was made by this child until after the documentary meaning that Michael Jackson would have had to commit these crimes after the documentary aired.

One good thing that the media did do for Jackson is, with the overplaying of Michaels settlement in the first case, Michael would learn from that and would not make the same mistake twice.

2003, Jackson would once again be charged with molesting of another child this time it would be 13yr old boy Gavin Arvizo aka the "Accuser." This time the charges were much more than just molestation; four counts of molesting a minor, four counts of intoxicating a minor, one count of abduction, and one count of conspiring to hold the boy and his family captive at his 2,700-acre Neverland Ranch.

Before the police, were even approached with this new allegation, the mother of Gavin Arvizo would first go to a lawyer, oddly, it was the same lawyer that tried Michael in the first case. The lawyer would send the children to a psychologist Dr. Stan Katz who was the same psychologist in the first case. Katz would later say, "Jackson was not a pedophile but a regressed 10 year old."

The raid on Neverland, by the police that came because of these new allegations was more than a fiasco, and was in fact the largest raid put together in American History. More law enforcement officers raided Neverland, more than any raid on any murderer or serial killer. That display of force was, largely viewed as uncalled for and excessive. To add another twist to the media circus the district attorney would also open a website and invite anyone who had been molested by Michael Jackson or if they had information against Michael to come forward.

The case against Michael Jackson would bring to light some disturbing news about the Arvizo family. In 1998, the family was, detained by J.C. Penny security for shoplifting. The mother would get into a scuffle with security and would later file a suit against *J.C. Penny* claiming she was severely beaten. A psychiatrist would find that Janet Arvizo had cohearsed and rehearsed her children into the alleged allegation. Two years later, she added a charge to the *J.C. Penny* suit claiming that she was sexually harassed by one of the security officer for seven minutes.

Gavin Arvizo's real father had divorced from Janet around the year 2000 in 2002 the father, David Arvizo, would plead not contest to spousal abuse and a year later would plead no contest to child cruelty. He would later petition the courts in 2003 to have the restraining order placed on him lifted so that he could see his son Gavin and make sure he was ok after the Living with Michael Jackson interview aired. He claimed he wanted to know, if his son had been sexually assaulted. In 2004, he would say that Janet Arvizo had been a mental patient and be quoted in saying, "My children are routinely rehearsed by their mother Janet to do or say whatever she wishes."

Gavin Arvizo met Michael Jackson in 2000, when the owner of a comedy club, would fulfill Gavin's wish to meet the Pop Star. Michael Jackson noted for being an extremely giving person, especially when it came to children. Also, noted for his soft heart for kids with medical illnesses, would befriend Gavin Arvizo, who had been diagnosed with cancer. Michael paid medical expenses for Gavin, and made accommodations for the boy to get to his chemotherapy sessions. Michael would be rewarded for his acts of kindness, with allegations of molestation.

Everything surrounding this case, in this fans opinion, was a circus from start to finish. Michael Jackson was in Las Vegas when a warrant was issued for his arrest. He would leave Las Vegas and fly to Santa Barbara airport where he would **surrender** himself to police at the airport. Media released pictures of Michael Jackson in handcuffs, as they arrived at the Santa Barbara jail. This wise widely viewed by the public as an attack on Michael and an attempt to show him as a guilty man.

In 2004, a Grand jury indicted Michael Jackson without a judge, without defense for Michael or Michael Jackson being present. The Grand Jury would listen to the accuser and witness's testimony and evidence without cross-examination from the defense.

The trial was also a joke, and consisted of testimonies against Michael Jackson from former bodyguard, who had a long criminal record of robbery to include: Radio shack, a Subway sandwich shop, a KB store, and a Jack in the Box.

A house cleaner, which was convicted, of stealing a sketch of Elvis Presley, from Michael Jackson. Who also had claimed, her son, was molested by Michael in the 1993 case. Instead of going to the police sold her story to Hard Copy, and a chef that was discovered to have his own pornographic website.

As in 1993, the trial consisted of "reliable," witnesses from the prosecution, a child's claim that once again was under the direction of the boy's parent, this time a mother, and the media circus that deemed Michael a sick pervert, without showing the facts of the case.

Unlike the case in 1993, Michael this time would not settle out of court. The trial would go on for over a year, and Michael would see it through this time. On June 13, 2005, the jury would deliver the verdict of Not Guilty on all ten counts. Justice for Michael Jackson at last, or at least it should have been. However, the media even with a not guilty verdict would not give justice to Michael Jackson. They would continue to make a mockery of Michael after the verdict, and continue selling controversy for years to come, even in his death.

Michael Jackson would never recover the image that he had when he was a part of the Jackson 5, or the widely respected artist we would know in Thriller. His music will forever be with us, but his image left to argument and controversy in blogs across the internet. The media has done exactly what they intended to do in the first place; make money off Michael Jackson, by controversy. Again, I will say a controversy started by the media, and should the facts, have been reported, there would be no controversy. Perhaps Michael would not have had the "need to just sleep."

To the media I have a question since Michael Jackson was ridiculed, for letting children sleep in his room, does that mean that a person who shares a room with an animal, is guilty of bestiality. I know that question is ridiculous, about as ridiculous as the media's rumors and stories of Michael Jackson.

Walt Disney once said, "I love Mickey Mouse more than any woman I have ever known." So what does his statement represent? Walt Disney also created a theme park for children; does that mean he is a pedophile? Is Michaels love for Peter Pan and creation of Neverland any more different? I can tell you the difference, Michael did not charge for his park; I guess making his park free makes him a pedophile.

It is also worthy of mentioning, that Martin Bashir, would go on to secure a spot as co-anchor for the very popular news sitcom *Nightline*. Many of Jackson's fans believe that Bashir's success can be attributed to his controversial interviews, of prestigious, well-known figures, to include the late Princes Diana. In reasoning, we can conclude, Martin Bashir makes money by tearing people down and spreading controversial stories.

As kids, most of us enjoyed something called sleepovers. Our parents would allow us to have friends come over, or we would go to friend's house and spend the night with that friend, in the same room. As adults, we seem to have forgotten, that we did things like this. As adults we consider this behavior to be for children and no longer acceptable for adults. Even though, Michael Jackson was considered an adult by age standards, at the time of these accusations, we all know Michael Jackson did not have your average childhood. He missed most things average kids enjoyed.

We also know that Michael attempted to regain his lost childhood in his adult life. We know this because of Neverland, because of Michael's character and by his own admission. Looking at Michael in this way provides a better understanding of why Michael had children sleep in his room. Did I mention that Gavin Arvizo also slept in Michael's room with the boys' brother and sister with him? It is surprising, that the media did not put out stories of group molesting.

These allegations were they only two that every came out of thousands of children, the media has made these allegations the forefront of so much controversy. Instead pointing out the facts and holding these two families responsible for false allegations, they destroyed an innocent human being.

As adults, we forget about what its like to be a child and child things that were once acceptable become unacceptable, when we grow up, which, is a part of growing up, but what if someone refused to grow up. "*Toys R Us*," base their advertising on this very thought. Is it hard to imagine sleepovers? As adults, we forget and view sleepovers as unacceptable behavior for adults, even though we allow our children behave this way.

Many people, love animals more than other people, because they feel the animal does not judge, does not complain, just is their as a companion and loves them regardless. Is this belief odd or unacceptable? Is it possible Michael saw children this way?

Is it possible kids relate to Michael because Michael had a childlike behavior, and believed he could live his lost childhood through children? As an adult, even though I would love to have met Michael Jackson, would not sleep in his bedroom but as a child, if you asked me to have a sleep over at Michael Jackson's house what would I say? Probably the same thing any kid would say.

I have heard something interesting from a variety of people when asked about Michael Jackson. People have said, you can only hear the rumor about Michael Jackson so many times then you begin to believe it. That comment in itself is an admission to being brainwashed by media influences. To say that kind of comment, means that although, their were only two cases brought against Michael, ten years apart, that media discussed these two cases so much, it seemed like there were many cases against Michael.

It also means that we can take a fabrication of truth and by repeating it repeatedly, we can make a lie become truth. I believe this is how Charles Manson persuaded people to commit murder. Is their a difference from Manson to media influence?

I end this chapter by mentioning a song that Michael and his sister Janet made together, the only one they made. It came out in 1995 and it appeared to me, to be a response to what happened in 1993, but more importantly, it showed to me a family member that came to side of her brother in a time of need. To Janet Jackson the love and commitment, you have for your brother is remarkable and it showed us a little more insight to the Jackson family. The family the media never wanted us to see.

Please, if you have not heard the song "Scream" by Michael and Janet Jackson, I encourage you to listen to the song. The video for this song shows how Janet stood with her brother.

Shawn Henning

Drawing provided by Anthony Harvey of Sweden

THE ENTERTAINER

Music, videos, and dancing talent out of this world. Michael Jackson leaves us with quite possibly the best entertainment of this generation that will surpass time and be available for generations to come. Practically 50 years of entertainment, a legacy that will be enjoyed for a very long time. We all have seen the images of Michael as a young child performing with his brothers and we relive the infamous Moonwalk of *"Billie Jean." Thriller* a timeless classic, which made music history, along with other music videos, that were more like mini motion pictures.

"I think everyone here was a Michael Jackson fan. One of, probably if not the greatest entertainer that's ever lived…" Tiger Woods

"I can't find the words right now to express how deeply sadden I am by Michael's passing. We have lost a genius and a true ambassador of not only Pop music, but of all music. He has been an inspiration to multiple generations and I will always cherish the moments I shared with him on stage and all of the things I learned about music from him and the time we spent together. My heart goes out to his family and loved ones." - Justin Timberlake

We know the man had talent, and that is one area not open for controversy. His songs will forever be remembered, and his dance moves often imitated but not quite the original. The King of Pops musical talent and love to entertain cannot be denied. One of the most successful artists of all time. Although most of what is written in this chapter is already known as, a fan I feel like you cannot mention Michael Jackson without mentioning his music and his accomplishments. His make up artist was quoted on film in Michael Jackson's Take Two by saying "Bashir's will come and go but Michael Jackson will live forever," this is probably the truest statement I have heard and this chapter is dedicated to that thought.

The Jackson 5 is where it all began. I will quote one of the sources that I found that I thought best summed up the impact of the Jackson 5, "They were an international multi-media phenomenon who ushered *Motown* into its second decade with a stunningly fresh sound."

Jermaine, Tito, Jackie, Marlon and of course Michael Jackson, these five kids rocked the music world and stole the hearts of millions of people across the globe.

Who could forget the young Michael Jackson? A child who at the age of five would find his nitch in a music career that would rock the world. If we look at those pictures of Michael, as a child, we can see he was a enjoying every moment of what he was doing. Those performances were Michael giving everything he had to them. His smile and talent forever changed music, and in Michael's eyes, we could see a glimmer that was as if, he himself knew he would be great.

Watching those performances were an inspiration to millions of people and the whole world wanted to be him. Ben Gordy told Michael Years later that "…if you do this you will go into orbit." For many fans, Michael Jackson was already "in orbit," the minute he auditioned for *Motown*. Fans even back then were crazy about Michael and they embraced him and to this very day will not let go.

Michael Jackson...

Drawing provided Anthony Harvey of Sweden

The Jackson Fives' first four singles would set chart records. *Time Magazine* wrote an article in 1971 called "The Jackson Five at Home" in that article it would say, "…a group that in hardly more than a year-has become the biggest thing to hit Pop Capitalism since the advent of the Beatles."

Michael and his talented brothers would sing many great songs that would forever sit as classics, one of them included a Smokey Robinson song rendition *"Whos Loving you,"* Michaels version would sing it so well that Smokey himself was impressed by this kids talent. Songs like *"ABC," "I'll Be There,"* and *"I Want You Back"* that would take the hearts of fans forever.

The brothers would eventually start to move in different directions each one becoming a success at whatever they would do. Jackie would go on to run a Record studio, called Jesko. Tito would marry, and have three kids that would from their own group, "3T." Jermaine would go on solo as well but would eventually become involved with charity work and some political work. Marlon would take a break from show business, become a successful real estate agent, and become part owner for a cable network channel called Black Family channel. Younger brother Randy, would also have children, and open his own record label Modern Records.

Michael Jackson would start his adult his solo career in 1979 with his first album *Off the Wall*, which would win Michael his first Grammy. The album sold 20 Million copies and went 7x Multi-Platinum. *Off the Wall*, was inducted into the Grammy Hall of Fame in 2008. The world had gotten their first taste of Michael as an adult and they were not disappointed. The album would include songs that would become classics;

- *"Don't Stop till You Get Enough"*
- *"Rock With You"*
- *"Working Day and Night"*
- *"Off the Wall"*

Michael recaptured or attention with this album and there would be more to follow. It would become #62 on the best selling albums list

The world would not be ready for what was to follow. Much more than just an album, it would include a music video that would rival a blockbuster movie. His second adult album would shake the very core of music and break racial barriers. It was so well done it would touch not only fans around the world but even reach the President of the United States. Enjoy the ride as I take you back to the days of *Thriller*.

The originally released album in 1982 would have nine songs 7 of those 9 would be in the top ten charts all over the world to include "Billboard Top 100." The album had songs that again would rest in our hearts forever and become instant classics. I have listed the album and the seven songs that would top the charts are in bold print. Michaels *Thriller* album would win 8 Grammy awards.

- **"Wanna be Startin Something"**
- *"Baby be Mine"*
- **"The Girl is Mine (with Paul Mcartney)"**
- **"Thriller"**
- **"Beat It"**
- **"Billie Jean"**
- **"Human Nature"**
- **"P.Y.T" (Pretty Young Thing)**
- *"The Lady in My Life"*

Michael Jackson would say to his manager John Branca before the release of *Thriller* "I want to be the biggest star in show business and the wealthiest." The release of *Thriller* would cement his wish. The media before the album release would say that it would not sell many copies and *Rolling Stone Magazine* would deny Michaels request for an interview. Michael had these comments for the media "I've been told over and over that black people on the cover of magazines doesn't sell copies … Just wait. Someday those magazines are going to be begging me for an interview. Maybe I'll give them one. And maybe I won't."

Upon release of the album, *Rolling Stone Magazine* would rate it four stars with a touch of negativity in their review. Expected considering Michael Jackson's comment after they denied giving him an interview.

The New York Star completely praised the album stating, "There are other hits here, too, lots of them. Best of all, with a pervasive confidence infusing the album as a whole, *Thriller* suggests that Mr. Jackson's evolution as an artist is far from finished."

MTV would play a music video from a black entertainer for the first time in their history. Videos, *"Billie Jean," "Beat It"* and *"Thriller"* would show in regular rotation. Michael Jackson would rock the world with new fashion trends. Fans from east to west would take the stores buying up copies of the groundbreaking album. Reportedly, over one million copies were selling per week. Ultimately, *Thriller* would take its place as the number one selling album of all time at a record breaking 110 million copies. No album released since as even come close to that.

Michael would win the Album of the Year award, which was huge for Michael as he expressed disappointment when his album "*Off the Wall*," had failed to bring him that honor. Bigger than that though, he would meet the President Ronald Regan in the White House and later the Library of Congress would preserve the album to the National Recording Registry deeming it "culturally significant."

Thriller would be Michael's masterpiece and although he would release other great and significant albums, nothing he or any other artist would release would live up to this. *Thriller* was re-released including songs not selected for the original version and fans for generations would be witness to the greatest album to hit the music world.

In 1983, Michael would reveal to us just how great of a dancer he really was. "The Moonwalk," Michael's signature move would be on full display in *"Billie Jean."* From that, moment on a new trend for dancing would take place. Although many people can do this dance now it will never be equal to Michael as he set the trend. Michael would dance as if he was the music and dancers all over the world have used him as the example of more than great dancing ability.

In the song *"Thriller,"* his dancing capability would again entertain us as we watched his magic in him, and the choreography. A dance commonly used in Hollywood movies, weddings and street dancing. Michael's dance truly showed a love for what he did and a passion for music that we know he had since he was a child.

Michael's moves were original. Often times we see entertainers that imitate other entertainers but Michael from his dance to his fashion was original. When we see someone doing the "Moonwalk," we judge it by Michael's ability and we say yes or no if it was like Michael. Michaels dancing was more than entertaining it is a style of dance that will echo the music world forever.

In 1984, the Jackson 5 would reunite and go on tour to follow their recently released album *Victory*. Michael would take a break from his solo career and join his brothers on the album and on tour. It was a moment for reflecting and giving their fans one more moment with The Jackson 5.

1987 five years after *Thriller*, Michael would release another album. Considering the magnitude of *Thriller*, this album was highly anticipated. Again, a number of these songs would become instant classics. With this album, it was obvious that Michael was not finished shocking the music industry and breaking records.

Thriller had 7 out of 9 songs that ranked in the top ten of Billboard Hot 100. Michaels' latest album *Bad* would have five songs that held the number 1 spot on Billboard Hot 100. It was and still is currently the only album to have done that. The album would sell 30 Million copies and became the U.K.s 9th best selling album of all time. The album did not beat out his previous album but still went 13x Platinum and won Michael two Grammy awards.

Songs from this album would include memorables as:

- *"Bad"*
- *"The Way You Make Me Feel"*
- *"Man in the Mirror"*
- *"I Just Can't Stop Loving You"*

- "Dirty Diana"
- "Smooth Criminal"
- "Just Leave Me Alone"

Although this album did not do, the things *Thriller* did, many regard it as his best album and rates number 27 on the all time best selling albums list.

Dangerous would be his third album, released in 1991. As was becoming the standard of Michael Jackson more of this music would become instant classics and would come with music videos that were more like Hollywood premiers.

This album would rock the charts just as the first two did. The album would rate number one on the Billboard Hot 100 for four consecutive weeks. Also like his previous albums, *Dangerous* was highly anticipated. So much so that a band of robbers would steal 30,000 copies, before its release date, at the Los Angeles International Airport according to contactmusic.com.

Again, it would not come close to *Thriller* as far as record sales and crossing racial barriers but this album would help Michael to achieve the Grammy's Living Legend Award. It was also help stretch Michaels Legacy from the U.S. to Australia from Canada to New Zealand. Michael was virtually in every country across the world with this albums release.

His music videos would be extravagant as always and the dancing would be more than exceptional. His videos would include Hollywood actors and athletes like, Macaulay Culkin, Eddie Murphy, Irving "Magic" Johnson, Tyra Banks, and Naomi Campbell. The album would be Michael Jackson's 2nd best selling album and make # 17 on the list of all time best selling albums.

Album songs would include:

- "Jam"
- "In the Closet"
- "Remember the Time"

- "Heal the World"
- "Black or White"
- "Who Is It"
- "Will You Be There Dangerous"

With only his third album as an adult Michael had been dubbed the King of Pop and there would be more to come from Michael as he still had more to contribute to the music world. *HIStory* would be his next album, released in 1995.

The album was a double disk that would feature 15 of Michael's best songs on the first disc. Disc 2 would be the latest songs from the King of Pop. Again, the Album would top the charts and hit number one in 19 countries around the globe. In keeping with classic Michael, that we have all come to enjoy, his videos would be as always, mini-movies.

Once again, many of his songs would be instant classics that would last in our hearts forever. Songs such as:

- "Scream"
- "They Don't Care About Us"
- "Earth Song"
- "You Are Not Alone"
- "Tabloid Junkie"

It would make the Best Selling album list at number 61. The album would sell 20 Million copies across the world and probably would have sold more but it was pulled from the shelves in the U.S. due to Michael's controversial song *"They Don't Care About Us."*

While on his *HIStory* tour, Michael would begin recording for his next album. The album *Blood on the Dance Floor,* composed mostly overseas was supposed to be a promotion for the leg of His European tours it did not receive much press in the states. However, even with little promotion the album would become the best selling remix album of all time. It would also top the charts at number 1 in 10 different countries.

The album would contain five new songs and eight remixed songs from his *HIStory* album. Even though the album was not highly publicized, it contained Michael the way we have come to know him. He would have horror writer Stephen King give him a hand to make the video *Ghosts*. His dancing and choreography still very much amazing. The albums new songs would include; Is it *"Scary"* and *"Blood on the Dance Floor."* Maybe, not the instant classic as his previous albums, but the album received less publicity than his other albums.

Michael Jackson's final album *Invincible* would be released in 2001. Due to some contractual issues the album was not highly publicized but still did very well in the charts, toping number one with Billboard Hot 100 and going 2x Platinum. The album would feature popular artists like Notorious Big, R.Kelly, and Babyface. The album would sell over 10 million copies despite the lack of publicity.

Again, for those of us that know what Michael meant to the world of music, the dancing and extravagant video making would yet again be on display in his final album. He would include actors Chris Tucker, Marlon Brandon, and Michael Madsen in his video *"You Rock My World."* Again, we hear great music from the King of Pop songs such as:

- *"You Rock My World"*
- *"Unbreakable"*
- *"Butterflies"*
- *"Cry"*
- *"You Are My Life"*

Michael Jackson through the years would give the music world countless videos and songs that future generations would use for inspiration. For his fans, we have endless memories of great music, fantastic music videos, and dancing that would influence the way we move on the floor for an eternity. His style would make a mark not only on us but also in the way we feel and think. It would call to us to change not only ourselves but also the world around us... From his song, "*We Are the World*," to his Heal the World Foundation, Michael Jackson truly gave the world much more than music.

His status as an entertainer for lack of better phrasing, the title of simply the best seems to fit. His mark as a humanitarian is without question. Michael's legacy is more than what any media personality can dream of having. With all that has been said and all that has been done to damage this tremendous artist and genius his fans around the world know Michael for what he was to music and to the world and the media can not touch his legacy.

"We lost a great entertainer and a pop icon. My thoughts and prayers go out to Michael Jackson's family, friends, and fans." - Arnold Schwarzenegger

Michael Jackson more than the greatest entertainer, he was also a man whose influence inspired change in so many ways. From breaking racial barriers to his continuing efforts in making the world, a better place to his contributions to children around the world. Michaels music is timeless but his contributions for humankind are more than remarkable and worthy of recognition.

"I would not be the artist, performer, and philanthropist I am today without the influence of Michael." Jackson, he said, "transcended the culture. He broke barriers, he changed radio formats. With music, he made it possible for people like Oprah Winfrey and Barack Obama to impact the mainstream world. His legacy is unparalleled Michael Jackson will never be forgotten." - Usher

Drawing Provided by *Ioana Cristina Zbantz of Romania*

THE HUMANITARIAN

"*Great minds discuss ideas; Average minds discuss events; Small minds discuss people...."Eleanor Roosevelt*

Remember always that you not only have the right to be an individual, you have an obligation to be one..... " *Eleanor Roosevelt*

The medias' coverage of Michael Jackson's death has opened up another controversial topic. Many people have regarded the coverage of Michaels death as excessive and some have even said Michael was not worthy of all the attention. To me the world lost not only a great entertainer but also a true humanitarian who has single handled made more contributions to society than most entertainers combined. For that fact, most politicians have not contributed as much as Michael Jackson has.

The fact that Michael Jackson is quite possibly the greatest entertainer that the music industry has had is enough to warrant some media coverage in his passing. Then if you add in his humanitarian efforts, the racial boundaries that he broke and the love from his millions of fans across the globe you can understand the necessity for the media coverage.

I am not saying that the media has accurately covered Michael infact most of the stories they put out even in his death are surrounded by controversy I am merely saying that coverage of Michael Jackson is warranted. I mention the medias' coverage because some views have been expressed about the medias' coverage, that were rather harsh and in some cases very slanderous.

Although the media has presented a view that did not display facts, Michael Jackson was more than an electrifying entertainer. His humanitarian efforts with the combination of his talent explain why his death was largely covered.

This portion of my book is dedicated to eliminating close-minded viewpoints that have been expressed. Although Michael Jackson was proven innocent in a court of law, it has not been enough to remove a label that he should never have had. Slander is defined by Webster's an "untruthful statement made that hurts a persons reputation or standing in the community." Example, if a person is proven, innocent then you cannot make remarks that say otherwise, that is slander.

Education is the key to understanding and overcoming prejudice opinions and stereotypes. I dedicate this section to educating those who may not know what Michael Jackson stood for. If we all could be like Michael Jackson, I guarantee our globe would not be in the state that it is in now.

Humanitarian is defined by the free online dictionary as "One who is devoted to the promotion of human welfare and the advancement of social reforms." Michael Jackson is the very essence of the word Humanitarian.

Well-known contributions of Michael Jackson include his songs:

- *"Heal the World"*
- *"We Are the World"*
- *"Earth Song"*
- *"Man in the Mirror"*
- *"They Don't Care About US."* (Social reform).

However, much more, than just music Michael lived his life in helping to save the world. His Heal the World Foundation is an active organization committed to progress and saving lives.

Michael Jackson contributed his time, his money, and his life into seeking change and making the world we live in, a better place. Michael Jackson cared about the world we live in, children around the globe, and for the soldiers that suffered injuries from war.

He spent time visiting our soldiers, donating money to the hospitals that cared for them. He also supplied new beds and other medical supplies. Not very many people can lay claim to doing the same. Critics of Michael Jackson have not invested nearly as much time, personal money, or energy into healing our world including care for our wounded soldiers.

Another focus of the media has always been about Michael's debt, but in the controversy of his finances. Why does the media, not discuss how much money Michael gave to the belief of making a difference? Michael supported at least 36 different charities in his life. I did not find out how much he gave to these charities but given the facts that Michael spent lavishly on things he loved. The fact that "Healing the World," was something he invested a lot of time into, and the fact that some of these charities were small when Michael started donating and are now quite successful. We could speculate that the amount was more than a small contribution.

I have listed these charities for several reasons. The main one is so that we can see Michael's commitment to giving back and healing. I also wanted to show the kinds of organizations he was committed to, the media would have us believe Michael hated his skin color and wanted to bleach it. I get a different idea when looking at the charities he supported.

- Aids Project LA
- American Cancer Society
- Angel Food
- Big Brothers of Greater Los Angeles
- BMI Foundation INC

- Brotherhood Crusade
- Brotman Medical Center
- Camp Ronald McDonald
- Child Help U.S.A
- Childrens Institute International
- Cities and Schools Scholarship Fund
- Community Youth Sports & Arts Foundation
- Congressional Black Caucus
- Darker Foundation
- Dreamstreet Kids
- Dreams Come True Charity
- Elizabeth Taylor Aids Foundation
- Love Match
- Make a Wish Foundation
- Minority Aids Project
- Motown Museum
- NAACP
- National Rainbow Coalition (Social Change for workers, women and people of color)
- Rotary Club of Australia
- Society of Singers
- Starlight Foundation
- The Carters Center Atlanta Project
- The Sickle Cell Research Foundation
- TransAfrica Forum
- United Negro College Fund
- United Negros College Fund Ladders of Hope
- Volunteers of America
- Watts Summer Festival
- Wish Granting
- YMCA 28th Street Crenshaw

With his music, his time and his money, and even his home Michael truly loved the world and made an effort to change things in and around our world. Senator Sheila Jackson proposed to secure Michael Jackson as an American Legend because of all he has done. However, because of the medias' image of Michael, this effort by Sheila Jackson is being met with opposition. If not for the speculation and rumors, Michael Jackson would be honored, the way is supposed to be.

If the media spent a quarter of the time they did in spreading controversy and just stating the facts Michael Jackson would be honored in a way that he deserves. Although this man deserves this honor as well as several others to include being recognized as a humanitarian his legacy is left for controversy in blogs across the internet and in the media vulture circus.

We have come so far as a nation and yet we take a step back when we allow this to continue. In my opinion to define Michael as a pedophile despite the facts is inaccurate and slanderous. Its stead of talking about what we think, shaped by media coverage, let us talk about what is fact. Pedophile, hardly please remember the court ruled innocent of all charges. Acts as a humanitarian well documented but hardly given the publicity.

Prejudice and ignorance is outdated and we can no longer make excuses for it. We work hard to make strides in technology, medicine, poverty, and providing jobs and while we continue to push for cures of these problems, we cannot keep adding to the disease of prejudice, racism, and jealousy. These diseases have already claimed millions of lives and we cannot advance, until we find a cure for them.

Educate ourselves and our children warn them of these diseases and take proper steps to make sure that our children do not fall victim to these grievous diseases.

For educational purposes, I end this chapter with a definition.

Webster's Dictionary defines prejudice as "an adverse opinion or learning formed without just grounds or before sufficient knowledge."

Drawing Provided by Kristina Farkas of Croatia.

REBUILDING NEVERLAND

Although in the beginning of my book, I stated this book would not contain interviews of prestigious people. Well I did come across one individual who shared some of his knowledge with me.

Mr. Larry Nimmer, a defense witnesses and filmmaker with a documentary entitled, "The Untold Story of Neverland," now available on DVD. In this section, I will discuss some of the key points in our conversation and I hope that with his documentary and this book it will rebuild Neverland as the place it should be, majestic, beautiful, a place of pure enjoyment and fun at no cost to its visitors.

"Too many people grow up. That's the real trouble with the world, too many people grow up. They forget. They don't remember what it's like to be 12 years old. They patronize, they treat children as inferiors. Well I won't do that." Walt Disney

"Forget them all. Come with me where you'll never, never have to worry about grown up things again." Peter Pan

My first chapter, Childhood, was meant to dispel some of the garbage, we have heard by media, and give us a better understanding as to why Michael would accuse his father of abuse. The Allegations gave a better understanding of the actual cases against Michael much of which was public information but never given the attention by mainstream media. The Entertainer was a view of Michael's contribution to music and the world showing just how much Michael Jackson meant to the "business," and to the world. The Humanitarian was to show Michael as the giving caring person that he was contrary to popular media rumors.

Now I would like to look at another of Michaels work one that was important to him and his legacy. Rebuilding Neverland is a chapter dedicated to show what a magical place Neverland was, an image destroyed by mainstream media. With Michaels, passing it is important to rebuild that image and show it as it intended to be.

Michaels' home would not only indulge his longing to have a normal childhood, but he would construct it to be a place for thousands of children and adults to enjoy. Neverland is as much a part of Michael as his music. If you would take a trip with me to a Magical place, where you did not have to grow up, but you could be a kid as long as you were there.

1988, Michael Jackson would buy his home from golf course entrepreneur William Bone. Michael would construct the home he had envisioned as a child. A home where he could live his lost childhood and do the things he did not get to do as a child. While most kids dream of being Superman or Wonder Woman Michael would mold his home into what he wanted to be Peter Pan. A character that made the world believe there was a place that you did not have to grow up and that place was Neverland.

Neverland would have three trains that would travel around the home, it would also include:

- Ferris wheel
- Carousel
- Zipper
- Spider
- Sea dragon
- Wave swinger
- Super slide

- Dragon wagon (Kiddies roller coaster)
- Bumper cars
- Concession stands throughout the park
- A cinema
- Beautiful lakes
- An arcade
- Golf carts
- Candy room

It would also include a zoo that would be home to exotic animals like:

- Lions
- Elephant
- Monkeys
- Llamas
- Camel

Many other beautiful animals could also be found at this magical home. One defense witness I spoke with, who filmed a documentary about Neverland, told me that, "The home also included a gift shop were you could have anything you wanted at no cost."

People dream of having a home like this. It is not only the house of man, who longed for his lost childhood, but also a dream house, for people with great childhoods. Who among us would not want their very own amusement park? Who among us could honestly say they would not like to be the owner of a lion or elephant? Home gaming industries make billions of dollars selling portable game systems for kids and adults so I know for a fact that people around the world, would love to have their own arcade.

The public is used to seeing stars and their houses. T.V. series have made huge profits in their showings of entertainers and their extravagant homes. "*Life styles of the Rich and Famous,*" and "*MTV Cribs,*" have taken us inside the houses of huge superstars and showed us how these stars spend lavishly on their idea of a dream house. America and the world gets an inside peak and can watch on television and dream of how we want our dream house. Many of us may never be able to have these beautiful houses but we still dream to have them.

While television showed us what it was like to be rich, Michael would take his dream much farther. He would open his home and share it with us common folk. Children and parents from all lifestyles, sick or healthy, could come and literally touch the things we all dream of having. For a time children and adults could go, play, and just enjoy the day courtesy of Michael Jackson.

Unlike other theme parks, Michael would not charge for any of this. The cost of the park and the animal's upkeep, he bared on his own. Media would not mention how great of a gift this was instead they would tear him down by exploiting Michael's financial troubles. While most entertainers would sit back in their lavish homes and media personalities would go home and lock up their doors, Michael was giving back to the community and the world. Any child that was not well off, sick, or for whatever reason could come and spend a day in a world absolutely care free.

The media has labeled Neverland, dangerous for children, a dark place, home of a freak, even though Michael had never been, convicted of anything, and the charges against him more of a joke than an actual case.

I pose this question while the media made money tearing this magical place down what contributions have they made to society. Have the opened their homes to the less fortunate? I hope that their contributions include more than twisting stories of people, to line their own pockets.

> *"For every one finger we point remember, there are three that point back to ourselves," unknown source.*

Michael Jackson gave us something that was tangible something that was not just a picture on the TV. Something we could reach, see, and experience. With all his heart, his time, and his money, Michael is the essence of giving back. Neverland contrary to media fabricated stories was a magical experience where people if just for a day could go, play, and enjoy themselves without spending a dime.

Michael took a childhood story and made it real for us. We all have read childhood stories and wished we could experience those stories in real life, we dream of it, we make it real in Hollywood motion pictures, and we watch it again in our living rooms or cinemas with our children. We laugh and cry, and for that moment live in a different world.

Hollywood makes billions and billions of dollars feeding people fantasies and we indulge in it if only for a couple hours. We buy billions of dollars worth of toys and merchandise for our children and even for adults who collect them. We all have had the dreams and desire to be the characters that Hollywood makes come to life; if we did not Hollywood would not be the billion-dollar industry that it is.

We remember entertainers for the role they played in our favorite movies. Although no one remembers the name of the boy who played Elliot in *E.T.*, everyone remembers *E.T.* Despite not knowing his name, not many people can tell you that he played in many movies after *E.T.* One was a blockbuster hit with Brad Pitt. He will always be the Elliot from *E.T.* This movie is a classic because how many of us we had loved to have been Elliot flying over the city on our bikes with a being from outer space?

Arnold Schwarzenegger will forever be to us the "Terminator," despite what he does as a politician. Arnold has made some great movies but even when he was elected Governor, many newspapers would run a headline that would say The "Terminator wins," or variations along that line.

Michael Jordon will always be, remembered as the athlete who made us believe we could fly, hence the name Air Jordon. For proof of this, look at his logo. We all know his success as a businessman, but we remember him for his flight capability.

Michael was what we all secretly or openly aspire to be. He made Peter Pans story a reality when he made Neverland. Moreover, it was an amazing place. It was a place where a Hollywood picture came to life. Something that we could enjoy, without the cost of admission.

If we were to pay entertainers by measuring, what they give back so many entertainers would be broke. Michael Jackson on the other hand would never have had any financial worries at all.

Drawing Provided by Kylie Malchus of Utah

Michael Jackson...

Michael would leave Neverland in 2005 the once magical home that he had created and called home would be forever tainted by images that the media would give us. Michaels dream to have a place where a kid can be a kid, and adults could take a trip back to childhood, had been shattered by history making police raids.

Now, with his death, Neverland may never reopen, but we should remember what it stood for. Not as the dark place, the mainstream media has given us, but as the place, it was built to be. A place, where childhood stories and magic, came to life.

Fans around the world would love to see Neverland opened as a memorial much like the infamous Graceland and to us it would be fitting considering Michaels love for Elvis, his love for Priscilla and the closeness of the King of Pop and the King of Rock and Roll. However, this probably will not be the case the media went through great lengths to destroy a man with a pure heart and in the meantime they themselves will never come to close to doing the things that Michael has done.

The footage of the police raid on Neverland showed Neverland as eerie and dark, it gave the impression that they were raiding a horrible place where innocence was lost to some sort of monster. However, in a conversation, I had with defense witness for Michael Jackson, and established filmmaker, who was hired by Michael Jackson and his attorney Mr. Thomas Mesereau, to document Neverland; the image of Neverland is very different.

Mr. Nimmer went into detail about Neverland with me. He talked about the amusement park, the zoo, the landscape, and the beautiful lakes that were on the property. He said that the home would play music the kind of music you would find at Disneyland possibly Fantasia. He told me about the three trains that would take you around the home and the golf carts that were also available. He told me about a mini castle that was also on the property and then explained to me how everything their, was of no cost to the visitors including food and gifts. He described Neverland as a Disneyland like, Fancy, with a museum feel to it.

He told me about the police raid on Neverland, he also told me what they were searching for. "They were basically looking for anything containing pornographic materials of children." Although the police had raided Neverland like no other home in the history of police raids, and with the thousands of books that Michael owned the police took only one art book. Meaning this large-scale raid was for an art book.

When I asked Mr. Nimmer if he had met Michael he said, he had on a couple of occasions. He explained to me the first time he saw Michael was out a window at the Court House, and he thought he was a boy scout, because Michael had many patches on his clothes. He described Michael as soft spoken and gentle although he did say Michael appeared depressed with what was going on.

Mr. Nimmer's documentary shows Neverland in its splendor, and he goes over some interesting facts of the Arvizo Family. I encourage people to watch this documentary as it gives us a very different view than what we have heard from the media.

I also asked Mr. Nimmer about his interview that he had on Entertainment tonight as I was curious about his feel for this particular television show. I asked him if it appeared to him that, the station was trying to search for negative things regarding Michael. He told me "since Michael's passing, they did stay a little more positive than in the past, but he still got the feeling they were searching for the odd or unusual."

I wanted to thank Mr. Nimmer for his time, as talking with him provided me with very helpful insight into Michael's beautiful home, and more information about the case against Michael in 2003.

Should Neverland be closed, we will have lost something amazing. We will sacrifice a belief of unconditional love, which Michael had when he built it, and we will have done it because the media said it should be that way. No matter what happens to Neverland his fans know what it stood for, and it will forever be a symbol of the true spirit of giving and magic. A place one could go and for a time not have to grow up. Your fans thank you for showing us the meaning of the phrase "giving back."

Michael Jackson...

Photo Provided by Larry Nimmer

THE MEDIA

"*Cause the media is full of dirty tricks. Only God Can Judge me.*" Tupac Shakur

"*The media's the most powerful entity on earth. They have the power to make the innocent guilty and to make the guilty innocent, and that is power. Because they control the minds of the masses.*" Malcom X

This chapter is dedicated to mainstream media. It is my account of the media's disregard for facts concerning Michael Jackson. I will try to avoid naming the media personalities that destroyed Michael Jackson, because they have the honor in knowing how much of a hand they had in destroying an innocent man.

I will discuss some of the claims the media has made against Michael Jackson. I will point out that no matter what we know to be true, the media would support ideas that feed into controversy.

This book is my answer to the "unauthorized biography of Michael Jackson." A book which I have not had the displeasure in reading, a book that I refuse to read because it is embraced by the same media that spent the better parts of their careers in destroying Michael Jackson. It is more of the same garbage that the media has been feeding us for years.

The author of that book is entitled to his opinion as am I but I will no longer take part in opinions that I believe are wrong and contribute to destroying a man that gave so much. None of these false witnesses will get a dime of my money again. The media in my opinion and in the opinion of fans around the world destroyed Michael Jackson and some believe may have even helped in his death.

Normally discerning what is true and what is not, lie in the eye of the beholder, however, this is not the case when the masses are being feed information, by sources that are supposed to depict and report what is the truth. If we are made to consider something true even though everything we know points us to believe otherwise and are ability to trust reason is compromised this is called brainwashing.

One dictionary defines brainwashing as this; "The application of a concentrated means of persuasion, such as an advertising campaign or repeated suggestion, in order to develop a specific belief or motivation."

It did not matter the facts the media has repeatedly reported what they wanted to report when it came to Michael Jackson. Take the simplest detail about Michael Jackson and his disease vitiligo. In 1986, Michael was diagnosed with the disease vitiligo and many pictures of Michael would show that Michael indeed did have the disease. The media would dispute this in order to further the picture they wanted the world to believe that Michael Jackson was "a freak, a side show."

Vitiligo is a disease that results from melanocytes (cells responsible for skin pigmentation) dieing or not functioning. Typical treatments of vitiligo include creams and avoiding sunlight. (Creams much like the ones that Bashir would claim in is documentary where bleaching crèmes)

When Michael addressed allegations that he bleached his skin on the Oprah Winfrey show, he would reveal that he had the disease. At the time of this admission, little was known about vitiligo, his admission would spark vitiligo awareness. Despite the pictures as proof of the disease, despite being diagnosed with the disease by a doctor, and despite the treatments that Michael would undertake to fight the disease the media to this day blocks the truth with claims that Michael wanted to be white and bleached his skin.

In 1993, even the prosecuting attorneys would acknowledge Michaels vitiligo disease and even try to use it against him to win their case.

In order to buy the media's claims you first have to believe that Michael hated his own color despite the charities he supported, and that he bleached his skin to change it. Then you would have to believe that despite Michael Jackson's "We are the World," song, made to raise money for Africa, that he hated being black.

Then we would also have to believe that, Michael would go to great lengths to hide his skin bleaching treatment. We would have to believe that everyday, every time he went out in public, every show he did, every video he made, and every interview he gave; he would doctor his skin all over to fabricate the disease. All to cover up that he was bleaching his skin

I realize how ridiculous the media's claims are but nonetheless they still feed it to the masses. Michael Jackson was proud to be who he was and took aggressive stances on being black; we saw that with his statement *to Rolling Stone Magazine* when they denied giving him an interview. In addition, it was again made clear in is dedication of the album *Dangerous*, to a black youth who had been stabbed to death. The charities he supported are also an indication of the medias' disregard for the truth.

Not only would the media fabricate stories about Michael Jackson's skin disease but also they would and still do attack his sexuality. The media would put out rumors that Michael was a homosexual again to support their claims that Michael was molesting little boys. Michael's complete denial of this was not enough to dispute this rumor. Michael's videos with beautiful women some of which were very provocative would not be enough. Michael's marriage to two different women would not be enough even though both women claim that their relationships were filled with sexual attraction and lovemaking. Even Michael's three children would not be enough. The fact that no male has ever stepped forward to say I was Michael Jackson's lover still is not enough.

The media continues to promote this rumor and the funny thing is they have nothing to support it. They say Michael wore women's clothes this is their bases for contending that he was homosexual. Michael Jackson took styles from women's clothes and turned them into fashion for men. The white sequin glove was a huge fashion statement and I can think of many heterosexual males who wore it in a statement of fashion.

By this reasoning everyone who wears a bandana is a gangster, every man who has a pink shirt in his wardrobe is homosexual. Everyone who gets an idea of fashion from another person must be trying to be like the person that he or she got the idea from. It also means by this theory, that every man who wore the Michael Jackson zipper jacket is a homosexual. Sounds more like stereotyping than stating facts.

One definition of the word Fashion is this "make out of components often in an improvising manner." When people invent a new style of dress it is considered being innovative not of being homosexual.

Again, I am baffled as to how the media can continue with these stories and we allow it. Are we that intrigued by opinions and drama that we share in destroying a man who has done nothing but give?

Even Michael's children are not safe from the onslaught of the media. The first case of the children coming under the medias' gun was the incident of the "dangling baby." This was shown so many times across the world and the media would slow it down and make it very dramatic. Now lets look at this again with some common sense shall we?

How many people, as Michael would say, have tossed their child into the air and attempt to catch them? Well what if they missed when the child came back down is this bad parenting?

How many parents let their children play with the family pet? What if the family pet decided to attack? How many times to do parents inadvertently place their child in harms way and in doing so run a risk of something happening.

People please I do not defend this action by Michael but be honest, good parents have done many things that could have resulted in a child injury, or even death. Leaving your child in the bathtub while you answer the phone real quick could be considered dangerous.

Bad decision-making does not mean we are bad parents it means we are human after all and we make mistakes. I watched a program on one of Michael's biggest rumor spreading channels and in that program, it showed a mother who has twin girls and she makes these young girls compete against each other in pageants. One of the girls would say I do not like competing against my sister but the mother would still make her compete.

In the competition, the girl would freak out, begin crying, and run off stage. The mother still made her finish the show. During the show, the reporter would make a comment that the mother clearly had her favorites. I watched as the mother described her daughters she would say that this one is beautiful and knows how to win while the other well she's just there At the end of the program the reporter telling this horrific story would proclaim "we took a vote and we are all hoping for the other (the beautiful one) sister to win.

Although I really wanted to avoid mentioning the names of these media scandal artists, I have to mention one of them here because this story about the twin girls aired on Entertainment Tonight the same station who has put out the most controversial of the Jackson rumors. The twin girls to me was more a case for bad parenting more than Michael Jackson's holding a baby for a few quick seconds to show his fans his baby. Again not the best way to do it but we do not always make the right decision.

Michael's kids would again come into the media's attention when the media would portray Michael as weird because his children were masks in public. Again earlier in this book, I mentioned that we do not live the life of stars. Paparazzi and star stalkers take every opportunity presented to inflict their damage to superstars. If a child is less seen and hard to recognize then just maybe you may prevent your children from a possible kidnapping. Not to mention the mountain of press that comes with being famous. Is it so abnormal to want to keep these children out of the spotlight?

Do we have the right to condemn this act of wanting to protect your children? Many entertainers keep their children away from the camera is this an act of bad parenting? To me it showed a protective side of Michael but even this was placed as controversy.

Now with Michaels passing the media has consistently put the children in the limelight and have avidly discussed the children's future; who they should live with, how do they feel, is there a fourth child made as a result of a one night stand? Still we have not heard much from the children. Is it possible that they are mourning the loss of their father? Why can we not let this family work things out; a son lost, a brother gone, and a father that is not around anymore? Do we have to scrutinize every aspect of Michael's life even in his death?

I am sure that when the family decides they have news to report they will. Please let this family decide what is best for their family member. Speculation leads to rumors and those rumors are hurtful and again put the Jackson Family under controversy, which is my mind, is sick considering this entire family suffered a loss of one of the family members.

In Jackson's death, the media would show their lack of compassion and continued spreading controversial rumors. They have had no respect for Michael or his family in these dark days.

Now we hear that the reason for Michael's prescription drug addiction is the result of one single moment in Michael Jackson's life. I agree that it is a factor because he would be introduced to pain medications and prescription drugs and I do agree that this is what got his addiction started. In 1993, Michael would admit that he was getting help for this addiction.

However, I do believe that the media is overplaying the Pepsi commercial gone wrong. Do they expect us to believe that the Pepsi commercial is the sole cause for Michael's addiction? I am not buying it.

When people have an addiction and they get help for whatever the addiction is they go through a program and that program normally includes something called a support group. In a support group, an addict will be introduced to a buddy, and phone numbers will be exchanged. The reason for this is so that in the event that the recovering addict should feel he/she is about to have a relapse, and have the need to use whatever he/she maybe addicted to, he/she will call his/her buddy, and that buddy will intervene, and try to prevent the person from having a relapse.

Now relapse is when a recovering addict feels the need to go back to that addiction to call on it to help him/her get through whatever is going on. Addiction is a dependency on something meaning a person has become dependent on this for whatever reason. Research, mountains of it, would say that stress is the main reason for recovering addicts to relapse. The recovering addict would be put under stress, and call on his/her addiction, to help him/her to get through whatever situation they may be facing at the time when relapse is possible.

Researchers say that there are many causes for addiction. One is that, if a person suffers exposure to something traumatic, such as a painful injury, an addiction will start because the addict will become dependent upon the drug that took the pain away.

Now, if the cause of Michael's addiction to drugs was the Pepsi commercial incident and he sought help for it, then he is no longer an addict, he is a recovering addict. A recovering addict if we go by the research, which states a, recovering addict, is susceptible to relapse under conditions of stress. The addict's dependency will reach out and call upon the addiction, as it helped him/her to get through the pain before, it can do it again.

The media is very open in pointing out the cause of the addiction but they are not so open to point out why Michael a recovering addict, would fall back to this addiction. Again, stress is the main cause for relapse of recovering addicts.

What could cause Michael Jackson to be under stress for so long? Well I have an answer again I am not a doctor by any means but I have had stressful situations in my life, as we all have and I think common sense can point out stressful situations. I also do have some insight into addiction as I had a family member who was addicted to drugs, and he went through a help program. From time to time, I would go to his program, to sit in and show my support for him. Amazing the things, we learn.

Are accusations of child molestation stressful? How about being accused of child molestation when you are a successful entertainer? How about accusations of child molestation, when the case against you is a complete joke and you have lived your life to help children? How about accusations of child molestation when you're a successful entertainer who has dedicated your life to help children around the world and the case against you is fraudulent but the media makes you into some sick perverted monster and puts your entire family through controversy after controversy and you have to pay 22 million to a family that had a father who drugged his kid to bring crazy allegations against you because you do not have the health to go through a long trial and then again 10 years later face the same thing again and this time go all the way through a lengthy trial and beat it just to have your victory of finally being proven innocent without a shadow of a doubt be crushed by the media who would drag you and your family though controversy after controversy and force you to close your home that you had built because it is has lost they very reason for its existence? Does this qualify as stressful? Would this make a person want to "just sleep"?

If the answer to these questions is yes then we have a recovering addict who was under a tremendous amount of stress not to mention he was about to make his comeback tour. Although I doubt that added much to his stress level because Michael was an entertainer probably the only thing left in his life that had not been placed under controversy and many people would say that Michael seemed healthy and ready for this tour. The footage of rehearsals show Michael very much doing Michael. I am sure there was normal anxiety to returning to the stage after that long but this was Michael and he was comfortable on stage performing and making music.

The media has not only used the Pepsi commercial as the forefront in Michaels' drug addiction but have suggested it was also the cause for a plastic surgery addiction. Another one of their attempts to show

Michael was a "sideshow," to further their controversial stories and sell their opinions. Another rumor the media spread with no facts.

The media has suggested that Michael Jackson was not only drugs but also plastic surgery. Although many entertainers undergo plastic surgery to alter their appearance, the media has used Michael Jackson's changing appearance as a source to add to their Wacko Jacko image and speculations. They have failed to mention the real cause for his appearance change.

Deepak Chopra doctor and friend of Michael told the world how his friend had Lupus and Vitiligo, in an article by *People*. Lupus as defined by The Lupus site is "a chronic (long-lasting) autoimmune disease where the immune system, for unknown reasons, becomes hyperactive and attacks normal tissue. This attack results in inflammation & brings about symptoms."

The Lupus site provides a definition of autoimmune saying, "Auto means self, so autoimmune literally means that the immune system fights the body itself. Instead of fighting & attacking the bad tissues, such as viruses, it turns on itself & attacks the good tissues."

Symptoms of systemic Lupus include:

- Arthritis (swelling and pain of the joints)
- Muscle pain
- Weakness
- Fatigue
- Sun-sensitivity
- Hair loss
- "Butterfly" or malar rash (a rash across the nose and cheeks)
- Fever
- Anaemia
- Headaches
- Weight loss
- Discoid Rash

While the cause for Lupus is unknown, researchers suggest that it cause can be attributed to a variety of factors, genetics', environmental, and stress are all possible causes to the cause of this disease. Michael Jackson was diagnosed with Lupus in 1986, it was reported to have been in remission at the time of he was diagnosed. It is also important to note that Lupus can cause the disease Vitiligo.

1984, Michael goes to the hospital for third degree burns to his face and scalp. Michael undergoes plastic surgery to correct the damage from the third degree burns. The media now uses this one incident as the cause for Michael's drug addiction and reports of a plastic surgery addiction.

1986, two years after the Pepsi Commercial incident, Michael is diagnosed with Lupus and Vitiligo. Lupus is diagnosed as being in remission and studies say that it could take years for symptoms to actually show. Researchers also point to stress as being a cause for Lupus.

In the two-year difference between the diagnosis and the Pepsi commercial gone wrong, Michael Jackson would receive treatments for Vitiligo and we would see a small change in Michaels' appearance. His plastic surgery, for the burns he suffered would also alter his appearance.

Those are facts, now between 1986 and 2009, the facts are lost, and the world is left with media speculation, which with all their experts and analysts makes their rumors seam like facts. However, if we understand Lupus and Vitilago and how they work, then look at Michael Jacksons' appearance and behavior we can use reason to understand that the media again gave us an inaccurate portrayal of Michael Jackson.

Lupus is a disease that damages the body, skin and their affects are usually a gradual condition, and researchers say may be caused by stress. Now, if stress is a cause of Lupus; is it possible that if Lupus is in remission could a tremendous amount of stress cause Lupus to come out of remission? Researchers suggest that stress can induce many diseases into an active state.

Think about this has their ever been a picture of Michael in a wheel chair before 1986? Did Michael ever wear a mask or try to protect his body from sunlight before 1986? What about after 1986?

In 1993, Michael was placed under investigation and allegedly did not have the strength for a lengthy trial. A team of people would take control of the fiancés and court proceedings and advise Michael to settle out of court.

These diseases provide an understanding of Michaels' so called odd behavior and changing appearance. Understanding what they do to a person and how they are treated gives insight to his use of drugs and painkillers. The media has reported so much opinion and controversial stories that somewhere along the line his diseases got lost. The effects of these diseases got lost but if you look at Michael and his behavior, it is clear that they match.

Michael claims in the Bashir documentary to have had only two plastic surgeries. The media disputes that by saying he changed so much, but they never point out what these diseases due to a person. They never discuss what role these diseases have on Michaels changing appearance or how sunlight affects these diseases. The media's only focus is on selling controversy and even now blames a Pepsi commercial for all Michael's problems.

They discuss his finances and the money he owed, but fail to mention how much he gave to helping or how much he shelled out on medical expenses for treatment of these diseases. In his death, has the media just once reported about the affects certain drugs could have on Lupus? According to one doctor, if a certain drug is administered by I.V to a patient with Lupus it could cause the heart to shut down.

Every facet of Michael Jackson's life was opened for controversy. Nothing has been left out. The media has twisted stories to make them suitable for their needs; they have added to or taken away and in some cases told false stories to support their controversial topics, in order to keep making money.

The circus is still not over, we still here stories of Michael's kids not even being Michaels biological children. Its funny how after his death how many stories come and with all this talk there is no proof of anything.

Drawing Provided by Anthony Harvey of Sweden

Just for a second let us indulge the media, let us say that the kids are not his. One question, is that our business? Michael raised them, lived with them, and took care of them and my book that makes him the father. All these people claiming to be the father, where were they when Michael was alive? Now, that there is money to be given, for the care of these children. All the sudden we have would be parents coming out of all kinds of cracks in the ceiling. Imagine that.

Of course, all this is just a fans point of view, although, I have done extensive research, my opinion is just an opinion of a fan. I do think that Michael was badly displayed by the media and in my soul feel as if they should share in the blame of Michael's death. Michael was hurt by the way, the media had portrayed him, his family, and even more disgusting than that is they have not stopped. Enough is enough.

Earlier in this book, I mentioned a song by Janet and Michael Jackson, a song that showed them standing together. I would like to ask the readers to see how the media affected Michael Jackson's music. Please indulge me and listen to the song *"Tabloid Junkie,"* by Michael Jackson.

STATEMENT

These pages are my formed opinion based on facts that I discovered in my search for the truth regarding Michael Jackson. Although close-minded individuals may pass of this book as mere ranting of a fan, I do encourage those who seek the truth to read and search for it. Not all that we have heard about Michael is the truth and much like this book, mere opinions.

I found so much in my study of Michael Jackson that was not openly discussed, like the Pepsi commercial gone wrong. So much that was not touched on, that would have given a complete different image of Michael, if the facts had been brought to light. It's like in Hollywood Movies when you hear the scary music in a horror movie you know danger is coming. This is what the media did for Michael they told his life, with the scary music playing in the background, and gave an image of danger. Shut the antics off and listen to the real story and you will see by reason that there is an entirely different story here.

We lost something valuable when we lost Michael Jackson, of course the music and the entertainment but much more than that. We lost a person who actively gave so much to healing the world; we lost someone who beckoned us to look inside ourselves, because that is where change starts. More than that, though we condemned a man because of baseless allegations and media stories and we allowed it to continue for years. Yet we have the audacity to be surprised to learn Michael Jackson was addicted to drugs and had a "need and want to just sleep."

Simply put, I believe that Michael had two diseases that affected his appearance and caused him suffer weight and hair loss. The media caused Michael an undue amount of stress with rumors, lies, and speculations. The alleged accusations by kids, whom Michael befriended and supported with money and care, turned greedy and repaid Michaels kindness with scandal. Eventually causing, Michael, to move from his dream home to a different country. Then you add doctors and greed into the mix with powerful sedatives, well logic will give us an understanding as to what happened to Michael Jackson.

Stress, is a huge factor in our lives, we are always warned about adverse affects that stress can cause. Michael Jackson gave too much of himself to a world that returned these acts with scandals. It is not the first time this kind of atrocious behavior as been allowed and I expect it will not be the last.

To know the truth about Michael Jackson we have to understand his love for life and the world, we have understand that he was a child at heart because of a childhood that he missed and longed for. We have to understand his, diseases and what affects they had on Michael Jackson. Finally, we have to turn off the media antics and horror music, and think about our own children. How would we feel if it was them in the medias' scope?

If we do not demand are media to report just the facts then we continue to make room for this to happen again and there is no telling how many times this has happened already. Opinions are not news, opinions can some times be hurtful and cause pain to an individual even scar that individual, we teach this concept to our children in schools. When do we teach it to the media, ones that are hired to report news and give us the facts? We do not need an opinion we have the ability to form our own opinion once we have the facts.

Opinions lead to rumors, jealousy, and more prejudice, they have no place in the newsroom, leave that for talk shows and blogs on the internet. I ask those who believe that Michaels legacy be kept intact and not left, in the hands of media reports and blogs on the internet, to please contact your mayor or congressional representative and help push Sheila Jackson's proposal to have Michaels' legacy honored the way it should be.

Michael Jackson...

Drawing Provided by Anthony Harvey of Sweden

PERSONAL TRIBUTE

To the family of Michael Jackson your son/brother/father is missed by so many. The fans want you to know that we thank him and you for the years of entertainment that you have and will provide for us. We can only imagine the pain you all must be feeling right now but our thoughts are with you. Please know that we as fans will keep Michaels legacy as it should be no matter what.

Finally, to Michael Jackson, I hope this book gives you some peace the peace that the world would not allow you to find even though you loved the world more than anything. You once asked us if we would be there and Michael a million voices cry out with your passing that yes we are here.

You gave us so much, you gave the world so much, and it will never be forgotten. Your mark on the world is here and among your fans stronger than any media attempt to destroy it.

Your music will be timeless and your generosity will be an example for future generations to follow, you more than set the standard. You taught us that magic does exist and you helped us to reach in our hearts and try to fix the problems that we know exist. You have paved the way for anyone who dares to dream and trust your fans will not let that go.

Occasionally, an artist or entertainer comes along had has the ability to reach inside our very souls. These select few, posses the ability make us believe in what they are saying, we can feel it deep inside. Michael is one of these select few. His music was more than something that just played on the radio, it was music, which grabbed us and told our soul to listen. More than just music videos, he displayed a clear message. That message was simple; the world is in need of healing, and love. His actions contrary to popular media opinion showed us how to heal the world.

Michael Jackson reached into the souls of people around the world from the U.S. to Kuwait and from China to Canada and beckoned us to believe in love and the power of it. It is hard to not be sad with a loss of this magnitude but something in us knows that you have found rest and peace and are among people who know the power of love.

Your music, extravagant videos and dancing will be, missed, as we do not have that anymore, it will not be an easy act to follow. We will take some comfort in seeing your influence on current entertainers and entertainers that will come. Most importantly, Michael your fans choose to remember you as the man you were and not the man they want us to believe. We love you more Michael

Thank you for everything.

Michael Jackson thank you for making me believe anything is possible.

In addition, I would like to thank the fans who have inspired me to write this. Our voice will be heard.

My loving wife who has stayed by my side through all of my tribulations without her I would not have been able to do this.

My mother for her years of encouragement and making me believe that I could actually do something like this. Yes Mom Elvis is still the King "uh huh".

My Family for believing in me and the message I wanted to put out.

ILLUSTRATIONS AND TRIBUTES

Michael Jackson's passing has had an affect on people around the world. Websites across the internet are filled with fans who have expressed their grief in a number of ways. All the drawings you find in this book were donated from fans who expressed their love for Michael Jackson by their drawings.

This section is dedicated to acknowledging those fans who mourn Michael and who actively participate in keeping His Legacy, as it should be. I wanted to say Thank you for all your hard work and contributions to this book and helping to spread the truth about Michael Jackson. The rumors and scandals do not show what kind of person Michael Jackson was; instead, they only show what kind of people we have in our media.

Kylie Malchus provided the cover illustration and when I asked her to provide a small bio about herself this is what she had to say:

"My name is Kylie Malchus and I was born May 21, 1990. I currently reside in Draper, Utah and I am the oldest of three. I recently graduated from Alta High School and now want to pursue art. I first started portrait drawing in high school. I credit my teacher, my mom, and of course God for my talent. I draw people I look up to. That's why I drew Michael Jackson. Like many from my generation, I did not discover Michael's talent until after his death. Learning about him has inspired me to be more charitable. It is unfortunate that I could not fully appreciate the man while he was alive, but I am now proud to call myself a fan. R.I.P Michael."

Many fans submitted drawings to me and although I could not use them all it was beautiful to see how many people around the world have a love for Michael Jackson. I took a small bio from each of the artists that we featured in this book as they are fans of Michael and did this for no other reason than to give their tribute to Michael Jackson. Anthony Harvey wrote this:

"I'm a 21 year old guy living in Sweden, I've been drawing more or less since I was a kid, as a kid I always drew, and I loved it. I had so much imagination back then, during my teenage years, I drew very little on my free time. I mostly just drew in the art classes in school. I knew I was good in recreating pictures but I never even tried to draw a celebrity portrait or something like that. I did not realize I could draw portraits until I gave it my first real try in February 2009. I was 20 years old then. I regret that I did not try it much sooner, than that, but anyway better late then never, right?

I never really knew too much, about Michael Jackson, because during my childhood I mostly just heard negative things about him. I guess it was in the early 90's, that the media, started to turn on him when he was accused of child molestation. I never believed it and I still think he was innocent. I think it is horrible how the media treated him; he was such a great person who just wanted to do good things for the world. He was a fantastic entertainer, truly the king of pop, with so many wonderful songs. I have always been a fan of his music and dancing so I wanted to make a tribute to a legend that was worthy of him. It took me a month to finish my artwork of MJ, but I think it was time well spent."

Another of our featured artists is only 16 but posses a great talent and love for drawing. This is what she had to say:

"My name is Kristina Farkas. I was born in Croatia, in 17 April 1993. Ever since I was a little girl, I loved to draw, so now I am going to the art school in Osijek. I remember when I first saw Michael Jackson.

I was about 6 years old and I was thrilled! I do not think there will ever be another artist like him. I love his personality, his looks, his singing, clothing, dancing, and of course: his drawing. As a matter of fact, his whole appearance. Michael was a big inspiration to me. When I'm drawing, I fell as if he is watching me, and smiling to me. I hope he is."

Another of our artists who contributed their illustration had this to say:

Ioana Cristina Zbantz (September 13 1987)

Born in Romania Dambovita but I'm living in Italy

"I have been drawing since I was 4 years old. I prefer to draw portraits because I can express myself better through it, through facial expressions. I studied at Targoviste (RO) art high school for 4 years. I wish to become a designer or a make-up artist. I cannot live without music. My favorite singer is Michael Jackson. The first time when I heard about him is when he came in Romania 1992; I was just 5 years old. I watched his famous concert at Bucharest. I like MJ because he is the most complex artist I ever seen. His music it's very expressive, has powerful messages and it's not vulgar. In addition, I really love his dance moves and I learned to do the moonwalk. When I was 16 years, old I made body painting, of some of my school colleagues, and I turned them into zombie, witches, and animals and then they tried to do the thriller dance. I just love him and I cried so much when he died. Rest in Peace!

Fahad AlZayed another of our artists is from Kuwait. He contributed his rendition of Michael Jackson just as a fan of Michael Jackson. He is a professional entertainer and singer. His main passion is music and has always been a fan of Michael Jackson. More information about him can be found in the sources section of this book. He had this to say:

"Michael Jackson has been a major influence in my life and music. I am not by any means a professional artists and my first passion is music. I hope to help Michael's Legacy live forever and that is why I did my picture for him."

To all the artists who contributed thank you very much for your time and commitment to helping Michael Jackson's Legacy live on. It is a pleasure to have your additions in this book and wish you success in your art. All of you truly have talent and hope that you keep pursuing your dreams.

The artist's names are provided with their illustrations and I hope you the readers will take a moment and view their drawings at the websites I have listed in the sources section of this book. Again thank you for keeping Michaels Legacy alive and it is my hope that together we can continue to show Michael Jackson as the man he really was, now and forever.

To end this book, I leave you with a special dedication to Michael Jackson from an upcoming singer. He has provided me with the lyrics to a song he wrote for Michael Jackson and I encourage you to visit his website to hear this song and to learn more about this talented singer. I asked him to write for me a small bio and share any thoughts he may have with me. This is what he told me:

"Full name's Carlo St Jules Jr. Born in Brooklyn, raised in Queens. I've been writing rhymes since the 5th grade. At least that's as far as I can remember me writing. Started as a way to explain things to my crush, which I was not brave enough to speak. I've been a fan of Michael as long as I can remember. My mother told me she remembers me attempting to dance like him since I was the age of two. Couple of years ago, I downloaded every Michael Jackson song to see if there was a track from him, which I never heard. One track of his which stands out is "Little Susie." For many years Michael's Invincible album has put me to sleep. It's my favorite album from him, even though it's the most underrated album from Michael. My Parents and best friends we all love Michael. My friends and I get upset when people refer to him as "One of the greatest." To us, there was no greater than Michael. Time to time I mention Michael in my songs. Like in my RIP Charlene track, I say, "Like Michael Jackson's song, You are not alone." Charlene loved Michael as much as I do. I remember her correcting me on his "Man In The Mirror" lyrics. Michael has inspired me to work hard to help others. That's why I'd never be a wealthy man. My money will always go to those in need. Like I always say, "Show me the world's richest man, and I'll show you the world's most selfish."

Michael Jackson...

Stay with Me
By Carlo St Jules Jr.

Brother and sister together we'll make it through
Some day a spirit will take you and guide you there
I know you've been hurting, But I've been waiting to be there for you
And ill be there just helping you out
Whenever i can
(Everybody's Free) Everybody's Free
Stay with me, Don't fall asleep too soon
The angels can wait for a moment
Come real close, Forget the world outside
Tonight we're alone, It's finally you and I
I Imitated you since the age of two
To say that you the greatest to hit the stage is true
Undebatable, Way you move, Only Michael J can do
Prayed that you would make it through
when I heard that breaking news
Naked truth, Dying, I'm afraid to do, Same as you
Today is too early to be taking you, Way too soon
Face the truth, There is no replacing you
Lived a life dedicated to you and I
Fans committed suicide, When they heard that you had died
You were a part of me, Now you're gone, Who Am I?
Wish you would've told them Angels Heaven Can Wait
Michael Jackson, Memory Stays, Never replaced
Pray that he is sent to us, Play that beat and dance for us
The day he abandoned us, Just to see the man above Man Above
Can't be real, This is just a bad dream, I can't wake up Can't Wake Up
Basically, I can't adjust, Can it be? Why can't you just
Michael Rest In Peace, You have left a legacy
What's stressing me is even in death they won't let you get some sleep
Words can't express what you meant to me
But I'll try me best to address just how special he
Was to the humanity, Not only music but especially
His contributions to the children from his charities
He's Donated 300 Million to take care of the

Hungry, the dying, and the sick. Incredibly
He created Never Land to give the kids a second chance
But some used it to take advantage of the man lent a hand
And Since you died on 6-2-5
I lost a part of me, Miss You Mike
What's worst is they turned your wake to a circus
Never heard of tickets for a wake being purchased
Vultures, Tryna profit off your death on purpose
Worthless gold diggers, Lower than the dirt is
Some people throwing dirt on your name like a casket
As if they tried to bury you before you died, Bastards
Negative words towards Michael Joseph Jackson?
Yeah, It's been heard, But, Thing is no one's asking
An icon is how I'd rather remember you
It is truly sad to see the crap that we've put him through
People say your death was a tragedy, And it's true
Prayers go out to your family members too
Janet and Jackie, Latoya, and Rebbie
Tito, Jermaine, Marlon, Randy
Joseph and Katherine, No Michael Jackson?
For real, It sounded so surreal when it happened
Pray that he is sent to us, Play that beat and dance for us
The day he abandoned us, Just to see the man above
Can't be real, This is just a bad dream, I can't wake up
Basically, I can't adjust, Can it be? Why can't you just
They say your entire life flashes by as you die
Now you're in the after life, But I'm alive
Asking why he had to die after I, Fell to my knees,
Begging you please, Spare him for me, Fact Is I
Sat and cried. All I know is that I tried
Guess I'll never see that Action Live from the Jackson 5
The first sound of Beat It! That gets me hype
He's a Bad man, Believe It, Ask Wesley Snipes
Used to play that Moonwalker game on Sega Genes
You broke every record like your middle name is guiness
Part of me feels that there's still a chance
That you'd awake from the dead like the thriller dance

Michael Jackson...

Your performance at Motown, Broke Grounds
Threw away the black hat, It's about to go down
Moonwalk, True Art, Life Lived, Too short
Who thought, You would end up like this, Huge Loss
New York, 2001,
You reminded everyone, Who exactly you are
Been performing live, Since the age of five
If you were alive, You'd make songs so that the issues would subside
Like, We are the World, Man in the Mirror
They don't really care about us, Earth Song, And it goes on
Biggie once said something that is real true
You're nobody 'til somebody kills you
But, Dead or alive, You were still a symbol
King Of Pop, Still you. Come back, Will You?
Pray that he is sent to us, Play that beat and dance for us
The day that he abandoned us, Just to see the man above
The starving children and women, It gets to me
But If Michael Jackson was living, He
Wouldn't Let This Be No, Nooo

ARTISTS SOURCES

http://lildevilme.deviantart.com/gallery/ (Ioana Cristina Zbantz)

http://www.youtube.com/user/loaded88 (Anthony Harvey)

http://www.youtube.com/user/KylieWyoti (Kylie Malchus)

http://www.youtube.com/user/TheGirlIsS0Danger0us (Kristina Farkas)

http://www.youtube.com/user/bskot80 (Fahad AlZayed)

http://www.myspace.com/cameo186 (Carlo St Jules Jr)

OTHER SOURCES

http://bumpshack.com/2009/06/25/celeb-quotes-on-michael-jacksons-death/

http://www.amazon.com/Michael-Jackson-Conspiracy-Aphrodite-Jones/dp/0979549809/ref=pd_sim_b_1

http://larryfire.wordpress.com/2009/07/01/did-stephen-king-and-michael-jackson-ever-collaborate-together/

http://larryfire.wordpress.com/2009/07/01/did-stephen-king-and-michael-jackson-ever-collaborate-together/

http://www.foxnews.com/story/0,2933,77884,00.html

http://classic.motown.com/artist.aspx?ob=ros&src=lb&aid=23

http://en.wikipedia.org/wiki/La_Toya_Jackson

http://en.wikipedia.org/wiki/Michael_Jackson

http://www.videocure.com/music-videos/m/d6499b91900ef1b2db35d04457846c05.html

http://www.brainyquote.com/quotes/authors/m/michael_jackson.html

http://thinkexist.com/quotes/michael_jackson/

http://en.wikipedia.org/wiki/People_v._Jackson

http://dianedimond.net/the-enigma-that-was-michael-jackson/

http://www.msnbc.msn.com/id/31553183/ns/entertainment-music

http://www.rockhall.com/inductee/the-jackson-five

http://www.penelopetalk.com/BOSS_ExecSummary.pdf

http://news.google.com/newspapers?id=Qo4RAAAAIBAJ&sjid=secDAAAAIBAJ&pg=2856,1082160&dq=michael+jackson

http://www.michaeljackson.com/us/home

http://en.wikipedia.org/wiki/Off_the_Wall_(album)\

http://en.wikipedia.org/wiki/Thriller_(album)

http://en.wikipedia.org/wiki/Bad_(album)

http://en.wikipedia.org/wiki/Dangerous_(album)

http://www.allmichaeljackson.com

http://www.theofficialcharts.com/album_chart_history.php

http://www.lyricsmode.com/lyrics/m/michael_jackson/scream.html

http://www.elyrics.net/read/m/michael-jackson-lyrics/tabloid-junkie-lyrics.html

http://www.highbeam.com/doc/1G1-97165467.html

http://edition.cnn.com/2005/LAW/03/01/jackson.trial/

http://edition.cnn.com/2003/SHOWBIZ/Music/02/03/jackson.bashir/index.html

http://en.wikipedia.org/wiki/Living_with_Michael_Jackson

http://www.guardian.co.uk/media/2003/mar/04/broadcasting

http://tvnz.co.nz/view/tvnz_smartphone_story_skin/166248

http://www.wnd.com/news/article.asp?ARTICLE_ID=30853

http://www.usatoday.com/life/television/reviews/2003-02-05-jackson_x.htm

The Insider

Entertainment Tonight

Martin Bashirs "Living With Michael Jackson

http://en.wikipedia.org/wiki/Martin_Bashir

http://www.amazon.com/Redemption-Michael-Molestation-Allegation-Unautographed/dp/0615306705/ref=pd_sim_b_49

http://thinkexist.com/quotation/recollect-your-thoughts-don-t-get-caught-up-in/357035.html

http://thinkexist.com/quotes/galileo_galilei/

http://www.flickr.com/photos/mushroom95/3694509336/

http://www.brainyquote.com/quotes/authors/w/walt_disney_2.html

Dozens of Michael Jackson videos courtesy of you tube

http://thinkexist.com/quotes/top/occupation/humanitarian/

http://www.people.com/people/package/article/0,,20287787_20288162,00.html

http://www.huffingtonpost.com/bonnie-fuller/the-real-reason-for-micha_b_221825.html

http://www.contactmusic.com/info/michael_jackson

ABOUT THE AUTHOR

    The author was born and raised in California, as a child at the age of ten wrote fo a local magazine entilted The Sun Runner. Later he would take a career as a defense contractor and move to Texas. As an adult he would travel the world and be recognized by Military Leaders for his work as a defense contractor. Now he returns to his passion for writing with a fresh unbiased view of Legend Michael Jackson.